VOLUME 10

PSALMS

David G. Mobberley

ABINGDON PRESS
Nashville

This book is printed on recycled, acid-free paper.

Library of Congress Cataloging-in-Publication Data

Cokesbury basic Bible commentary.
  Basic Bible commentary / by Linda B. Hinton . . . [et al.].
    p. cm.
  Originally published: Cokesbury basic Bible commentary. Nashville
Graded Press, © 1988.
  ISBN 0-687-02620-2 (pbk. : v. 1 : alk. paper)
  1. Bible—Commentaries. I. Hinton, Linda B. II. Title.
[BS491.2.C65 1994]
220.7—dc20   94-10965
                                                                      CIP

ISBN 0-687-02629-6 (v. 10, Psalms)
ISBN 0-687-02620-2 (v. 1, Genesis)
ISBN 0-687-02621-0 (v. 2, Exodus–Leviticus)
ISBN 0-687-02622-9 (v. 3, Numbers–Deuteronomy)
ISBN 0-687-02623-7 (v. 4, Joshua–Ruth)
ISBN 0-687-02624-5 (v. 5, 1–2 Samuel)
ISBN 0-687-02625-3 (v. 6, 1–2 Kings)
ISBN 0-687-02626-1 (v. 7, 2 Chronicles)
ISBN 0-687-02627-X (v. 8, Ezra–Esther)
ISBN 0-687-02628-8 (v. 9, Job)
ISBN 0-687-02630-X (v. 11, Proverbs–Song of Solomon)
ISBN 0-687-02631-8 (v. 12, Isaiah)
ISBN 0-687-02632-6 (v. 13, Jeremiah–Lamentation)
ISBN 0-687-02633-4 (v. 14, Ezekiel–Daniel)
ISBN 0-687-02634-2 (v. 15, Hosea–Jonah)
ISBN 0-687-02635-0 (v. 16, Micah–Malachi)
ISBN 0-687-02636-9 (v. 17, Matthew)
ISBN 0-687-02637-7 (v. 18, Mark)
ISBN 0-687-02638-5 (v. 19, Luke)
ISBN 0-687-02639-3 (v. 20, John)
ISBN 0-687-02640-7 (v. 21, Acts)
ISBN 0-687-02642-3 (v. 22, Romans)
ISBN 0-687-02643-1 (v. 23, 1–2 Corinthians)
ISBN 0-687-02644-X (v. 24, Galatians–Ephesians)
ISBN 0-687-02645-8 (v. 25, Philippians–2 Thessalonians)
ISBN 0-687-02646-6 (v. 26, 1 Timothy–Philemon)
ISBN 0-687-02647-4 (v. 27, Hebrews)
ISBN 0-687-02648-2 (v. 28, James–Jude)
ISBN 0-687-02649-0 (v. 29, Revelation)
ISBN 0-687-02650-4 (complete set of 29 vols.)

94 95 96 97 98 99 00 01 02 03—10 9 8 7 6 5 4 3 2 1

MANUFACTURED IN THE UNITED STATES OF AMERICA

Contents

Outline of Psalms

I. Book I: Psalms 1–41
   A. Part 1: Some Philosophic Problems (Psalms 1–10)
      1. Two Life-styles
      2. A Coronation Hymn
      3. God Is a Shield
      4. Inner Peace
      5. A Straight Pathway
      6. Justice and Mercy
      7. Let Justice Be Done
      8. How Majestic Is Your Name
      9. Evil Enemies
      10. Poverty and Suffering
   B. Part 2: What Is God Really Like? (Psalms 11–20)
      11. God's Law and Order
      12. God's Precious Words
      13. God's Steadfast Love
      14. God Is!
      15. The Presence of God
      16. God's Presence Is Joy
      17. God Hears People
      18. God's King Triumphs
      19. God's Universal Law
      20. God Helps People
   C. Part 3: Confidence and Serenity (Psalms 21–31)
      21. Prayers for the King
      22. Yet Will I Believe
      23. The Lord Is My Shepherd
      24. The King of Glory
      25. Teach Me, O Lord
      26. Test Me, O Lord
      27. A Courtroom Drama
      28. The Lord Is a Refuge
      29. The Voice of Thunder
      30. The Lord Is Gracious
      31. My Times Are in Your Hand
   D. Part 4: The Pursuit of Happiness (Psalms 32–41)
      32. Freedom from Guilt
      33. Secure in the Lord

Introduction to Psalms

Few other books of the Bible, except perhaps the Gospels, have influenced religious experience with quite the effect of the Psalms. Their poetry includes some of the richest language in the literary world, incomparable in power and loveliness. Reflecting on the quality and character of the Psalms, we are aware of their effects on countless generations who have turned to them for personal guidance. We cannot underestimate the strength in these beautiful lines, whether it be to find consolation in loneliness, despair, grief, and pain or to acquire knowledge and inspiration from moments of meditation.

Unlike other books of the Bible which are addressed to humanity and deal with the subjects of law, history, prophecy, wisdom, and instruction, the Psalms are addressed to God or are written about God. Within these 150 poems, a systematic theology is not evident. Nor is there any historical continuity or unifying religious theme. Nevertheless, throughout the Psalms, on virtually every page, the assumption is stated or implied that God exists, and that concept is never in doubt.

The core of the entire book is the wonderful awareness of God's presence. The deepest yearnings of the soul for an intimate, personal, and right relationship with God are apparent. In those yearnings the broadest range of human emotion is evident. Psalmists are dealing with deepest despair and highest elation, profound grief and supreme joy, utmost sorrow and greatest gladness. But they are also dealing with profoundly important moral and ethical principles. Throughout these poems, deepest respect for the law is apparent. It actually becomes the ethical ideal of the people of God's choosing.

At the same time the Psalms relate the story of the

Israelite nation, its high moments of exultation and supreme glory and its grim days of calamity and national disaster. The episodes have a timeless quality about them, appropriate to any period of history including the present. The glowing appeal of these stories is the almost continuous conquest of despair and the heart-warming victory of hope. As personal, devotional resources, these beautiful poems are most valued as deep springs of refreshment and renewal and marvelous sources of comfort.

Psalms and Music

The psalmists have created a great book of hymns which affirms both awesome power and tender personal intimacy as important traits of a monotheistic God. The people for whom the writers composed and recorded the poems are God's people who have drawn on the qualities of power and intimacy in those great hymns for twenty-five hundred years.

So, the Bible's hymnbook is the Psalms. Each psalm is superb lyric poetry that was, at one time, set to music.

Pipes, reeds, percussion, and strings such as the psaltery and lute were used. The English word *psalm* is derived from the Latin *psalmus* which meant the twanging or strumming of a stringed instrument. Verses 1-3 of Psalm 81 describe the degree to which music and poetry were related in Israel's early life:

Sing aloud to God our strength;
shout for joy to the God of Jacob!
Raise a song, sound the tambourine,
the sweet lyre with the harp.
Blow the trumpet at the new moon,
at the full moon, on our festal day. (NRSV)

Among the very early Hebrew peoples, hymns and songs were memorized in religious training and during social activities of community life. In this way, their best-loved poetry was passed from generation to generation. Bible scholars generally believe that some of the present collection of psalms was accumulated by means of this oral tradition over a period of many centuries.

From the earliest periods in Israel's history religious experiences were at the center of community life. Singing was a part of those activities. Psalms were sung during festivals, on national holidays and high holy days, and during pilgrimages to Jerusalem. As the Hebrews made their customary pilgrimages, they sang psalms of praise.

Titles of some of the psalms contain specific references to choirmasters and to Temple singers such as the Sons of Korah and Asaph. Hymns and anthems were used regularly by the early Hebrews as aids to worship, beginning a tradition that has endured to our time.

In one important sense the individual psalms are prayers, and in recognition of this attribute they are incorporated into denominational prayer books and psalters. The Psalter in the hymnals of most churches contains selected psalms usually printed as responsive readings. Also, frequent use is made of entire psalms or individual verses or sentences in hymns, canticles, collects, and other prayers and acts of praise.

Hymns in use in most Christian denominations include psalms which have been rephrased in rhyme to conform to the meter of traditional hymn tunes. Note how the lovely lines of the Twenty-third Psalm (King James Version) have been rearranged to fit one of several tunes in common use:

The LORD is my shepherd, I shall not want;
He maketh me to lie down in green pastures.
He leadeth me beside the still waters;

The Lord's my shepherd, I'll not want,
He makes me down to lie
in pastures green; he leadeth me
The quiet waters by.

The Authorship of the Psalms

Authorship of the Psalms is in dispute among biblical scholars, as is the question of by whom and when they were accumulated from the oral tradition. It is true that the Hebrew texts ascribe much of the poetry to David. Biblical scholars have suggested that some of the psalms attributed to David may be poems written by others for David or about him, or written using his literary style. Some scholarly opinion places authorship of many psalms much later in Israel's history, perhaps after the Babylonian captivity and up to the time of the Maccabean era. Recent evidence shows, however, that a number of the psalms may have been written or recorded at earlier dates than scholars has previously thought. In their original forms, many can be shown to date from the monarchical period of Saul, David, and Solomon.

Regardless of who the authors of these psalms were, there is no doubt that David is still the central human figure in the Psalms. His strong relationships with and his virtually unswerving devotion to God dominate the stories throughout the book.

Purposes of the Psalms

The Psalms were put into their present arrangement sometime before the era of the Maccabees (165 B.C.), probably 300–200 B.C. By the time of the Christian era, all of the Psalter had actually been incorporated into the Hebrew Bible, and before too long thereafter into the earliest Christian Bibles as well. Two purposes seem to have been served by including the Psalms in the Bible: public worship and personal devotion. In the first instance, psalms have important liturgical uses in religious services. Introductory statements above the biblical text of a number of psalms include specific instructions as to how the poem is to be used in worship or in celebration. Although the meaning of many of the words in those introductory statements is obscure, there is little doubt that they were directions given to the congregation to enable proper participation in the service. Refer to the Glossary, which lists these instructional terms and their possible definitions.

A second purpose served by the Psalms was private, personal devotion. The Twenty-third Psalm was evidently not used anywhere in liturgy among the people of Israel. But as a quiet, devotional, personal prayer it is incomparable. This and other psalms of comfort and confidence have shown unusual power in bringing people into a unique personal experience with the living God.

Literary Structure of the Psalms

The reader's enjoyment and understanding of the Psalms will surely be enhanced by some understanding of their literary structure. We should remember that the individual psalms are poetry despite the fact that they do not appear to have any rhyme. The original Hebrew did not have rhyme either; it depended upon stress during recitation in order to achieve poetic quality. It might be helpful to try reading some psalms aloud, accenting certain words to assess the psalms as poetry. The structure of the poetry is quite simple; it is comprised of line, verse, and stanza. The verses are usually numbered. When a verse has two distinct subjects or if its two parts are obviously related to two different stanzas, references to one of the parts in this and other commentaries will use the small letters *a* or *b* to represent the first or second part of a verse. Occasionally, verses will take the form of a beatitude, the first word of which is *blessed, happy,* or an equivalent.

As in all literature identified as poetry, psalms possess rhythm, meter, and a certain lyric quality. But these traits are not always evident. Translations have often sacrificed the original Hebrew metered stress and rhythm in order to achieve greater faithfulness in meaning.

Literary devices most commonly employed in the writing and the translating of the Psalms are word pictures, figures of speech, and parallelisms of three types. The first is synonymous, in which the idea expressed in one line is repeated with different words in the line that follows:

The snares of death encompassed me;
the pangs of Sheol laid hold on me (Psalm 116:3 NRSV).

The NIV reads:

The cords of death entangle me,
the anguish of the grave came upon me.

A second type of Hebrew parallelism is antithesis, in which the subject of the first line is followed in the next line by a thought that expresses an opposite or contrary idea:

My flesh and my heart may fail,
but God is the strength of my heart
and my portion forever (Psalm 73:26 NIV and NRSV).

The third type of parallelism is complementary, in which the idea expressed in the second line complements or in some way adds to the thought in the first line:

But I trusted in your steadfast love;
my heart shall rejoice in your salvation (Psalm 13:5 NRSV).

Abundant use of extraordinary and colorful figures of speech gives all the psalms special beauty and their lovely, lyrical quality. Often used is the metaphor:

He makes the clouds his chariot,
and rides on the wings of the wind (Psalm 104:3 NIV) in which things used in comparisons are quite different. Also often used is the simile:

He is like a tree planted by streams of water (Psalm 1:3 NIV) in which different words or things are compared and introduced by the words *like* or *as*.

The Psalms also contain some hyperbole:

Have they no knowledge, all the evildoers
Who eat up my people as they eat bread (Psalm 14:4 NRSV)

which is clearly deliberate exaggeration in order to emphasize a point.

Many of the psalms, especially the laments, are written in similar format. The psalms begin with a cry for help accompanied by a description of the cause of anguish. Often the cause is a false accusation but it can also be threats of murder, terrible illness, mental distress, or even national calamities. A declaration of trust usually follows along with an expression of confidence that God will intervene. The final words of these poems are thanksgiving for deliverance.

Within the text of a number of psalms, the word *selah* occurs repeatedly. It does not appear to have any literary significance and it has no known meaning in Hebrew. Some students of early music surmise that it may have been an instruction for singing, perhaps to indicate a pause in the liturgy or to allow the introduction of some special feature into the ritual.

The Plan of the Commentary

The general plan of this commentary is a treatment of individual psalms in numeric sequence from 1 to 150. For convenience, they are divided into sixteen parts. Because the poems do not follow a story plot nor any particular order by subject, the attempt to treat each part as having a general theme may seem somewhat artificial. On the other hand, one can find affinities among some of the psalms in each part. The introductory sentences for each of the sixteen parts provide some ideas about ways of focusing one's thoughts on a small group of poems which may be studied and understood in one sitting. The arrangement may also be useful for private devotions and for the preparation of teaching materials for lessons on the Bible.

Psalms 1–10

Introduction to These Psalms

The authors of the Psalms were deeply religious thinkers and supremely confident believers in God. Their beliefs were touched with a sense of awe and wonder in the presence of the Almighty. So it was that in the act of wondering, the deepest questions about the nature of God, humanity, and the world came to light.

Part One of the book of Psalms (1–10) deals with some rather traditional religious and philosophic questions: good and evil, justice and mercy, anxiety and happiness, as well as the sources of moral law. Also raised are interesting questions about the divine right of kings, the majesty of God, the nature of grace, and whether or not people can approach God directly as an intimate friend.

The importance of a philosophic attitude cannot be dismissed easily. We gain immeasurable insight by asking searching, penetrating questions. In our study of this part of Psalms the questions are the same as those which have perplexed Christians for centuries.

Two Life-styles (Psalm 1)

Psalm 1 deals with the nature of righteousness as it describes two contrasting lifestyles. Two stanzas of three verses each echo the age-old philosophic conflict between good and evil, between righteousness and ungodliness. The psalm asks us to choose the way of the godly person. As you read the first stanza (verses 1-3), consider the qualities of the righteous. Do the righteous heed those who recommend ~~wicked~~ ways? They have learned to be wary of beguiling, seductive pressures inviting them to ~~slothful~~, imprudent behavior. The blessed or the happy (verse 1) prefer not to stand among the ~~wicked who sin~~ consciously nor to join those who are scornful of the righteous.

Trees and streams (verse 3) are a picturesque way of calling attention to God's plan for all living things. When the environmental conditions are just right, it may be reasonably expected that life will be lived according to God's laws and purposes. The righteous are also marked by their willingness to refine and improve their understanding of the moral law, making such devotionals part of every day's activities.

The second stanza, verses 4-6, deals with the ~~wicked.~~ The psalmist uses a simple figure of speech, a simile familiar to every Hebrew family. The ~~wicked~~ are likened to chaff—dry wisps of grain husks that were wafted up and away from the threshing floor at harvest time. Unlike ripe grain, the chaff was of no value. The slightest winds blew it away. So it was for the ungodly without roots in the faith.

In verse 5, the ~~wicked~~ are judged unfavorably and are excluded from the privileges of earthly congregations of the righteous. The psalmist leaves no doubt about what will happen to the way of the ~~wicked~~ (verse 6). Condemnation of the ungodly life-style is straightforward and is sung with full assurance. ~~Evil ways are doomed!~~

A Coronation Hymn (Psalm 2)

Anointing a Hebrew king was a religious act, the high moment in the coronation ceremony. When one king succeeded another, the coronation was held in autumn at the time of the fruit harvest. The harvest was also the occasion for the annual Festival of Ingathering or Tabernacles. Autumn was the time for the new year celebration and the ritual of covenant renewal.

The psalm was recited by the new king during the anointing ceremony to stress the unique relationship between God and the royal monarch. The theme is God's appointment of a king. This divine act is derived from Nathan's prophecy to David (2 Samuel 7:8-12) in which God established David as king and provided for royal succession through David's lineage. Christian tradition holds this genealogy crucial in the ancestry of Jesus Christ.

The poetry includes four stanzas of three verses each. In the first stanza, the king tells the faithful that all the nations of the world are in deep trouble because they have rejected the universal sovereignty of God. In the second stanza the psalmist, probably the king, describes a scornful God laughing at the ridiculous plotting and scheming of the heathen kings. Their futile efforts will come to nothing; Israel's anointed king is to rule the nations. World government is to be established on Mount Zion.

The third stanza (verses 6-9) describes God's act of appointing the begotten son to become the king and putting the whole earth under divine rule. The anointed king was not considered to be divine, but because he became the adopted son of God, his authority was of divine origin.

The powers here bequeathed to David and a long line of David's successors came to have enormous political significance in the history of western civilization. Vestiges of the divine right of kings are still apparent in some parts of the world, although the idea that a monarch's rule was absolute has been discarded among the western democracies.

During the ceremony, the anointed king used the final stanza to advise the heathen kings to yield to God's authority before it was too late. Kissing the king meant kissing the new king's feet. That was considered a suitable indication that rulers of other nations would be ready to submit.

God Is a Shield (Psalm 3)

David is apparently the author of this psalm. It was composed during Absalom's revolt when David had determined, for the good of the nation and his own safety as well, that the headquarters of the kingdom should be moved out of Jerusalem. He may also have wanted to avoid battle damage to Zion, God's holy hill. David's decision to flee is told in 2 Samuel 15:14-17.

The first of the poem's stanzas describes the king's political situation. He is clearly beset by a host of enemies, and the number is growing. Among those enemies are heathens who seem to be gloating over the fact that God is not giving any help to David in his predicament. In the midst of all of this difficulty David offers a stirring statement of faith, affirming in stanza two his certain belief that God will protect the anointed king by being a *shield*. The metaphor of the shield alludes to the warrior's best defense in battle against the slings and arrows of the enemy.

Verse 4 reveals the extraordinary depth of David's faith: The Lord will answer the king's cries; the Lord will answer from Zion. And so, as the story in 2 Samuel relates, King David survived the crisis with Absalom and lived on through a successful reign.

Stanza three is a clear statement of faith based on God's simple gifts, those of sleep through a restful night and being allowed to awaken to a new day. Because God's support of people is that well-assured, ten thousand foes (probably hyperbole) cannot ever become a source of fright.

The fourth stanza opens with words that have the ring of a command: *Arise* (NIV; NRSV = *Rise up*) *O Lord.* *Breaking teeth* may well be a figure of speech for stilling the clamor of a battle and the voices of those who, as in verse 1, have ridiculed the king about getting no help from God. Verse 8 is the epilogue of the psalm. It is not an afterthought, but a vigorous utterance of David's belief that God alone has the authority and the power to protect the kingdom from its enemies.

Inner Peace (Psalm 4)

Here are beautiful words of assurance for a person whose honor has been shamed by slanderous words. Evidently the political situation in David's time brought about mudslinging in much the same way as it does in our time. In a careful line-by-line statement, David has defined slander and its consequences both to those who are slandered and to the wicked who have uttered the words.

The meter of the poetry is somewhat irregular, with eight verses of varying length and texture. The first verse is addressed to God as *God of my Right* (NRSV) or *righteous God* (NIV). This probably means the God who gives and sustains the rights of citizenship. The theme of the psalm (verse 2) is proposed to David's political opponents. It is a simple matter. How long will you continue to lie? Typical of the person injured by such slander, the honest and righteous David tells them the Lord has special regard for him and for all other godly ones. And because of that special relationship God listens.

Surely godly people may become angered (verse 4) by lies being told about them. However, that should not be taken as a license to sin in response. If that impulse befalls you, commune (pray) with God, continue to be faithful to your religious obligations, and trust in God. Is there any better recipe for inner peace?

Verse 6 is an admission that willingness to trust in God might be enhanced if one could be shown a sign to reinforce belief. Seeing the Lord's face would be sufficient.

David seems not to be confounded by such doubts. Even though his enemies are prospering (*abounding in grain and wine* is a useful metaphor), God has given him joy and peace as only a good and gracious God can do.

The entire psalm is a wonderful lesson for persons who have suffered because of the bearing of false witness. Is it possible to deal graciously with lies and liars?

A Straight Pathway (Psalm 5)

In this poem, David continues his prescription for dealing with those who persist in lying and spreading false rumors. The first of the poem's five stanzas includes two sentences of invocation followed by a reminder that God listens when faithful people say their morning prayers. The approach in stanza two changes to descriptive words about some of God's attributes as the wicked, boastful enemies are now getting their just deserts.

In stanza three, David prays to the Lord, promising to worship in God's house and asking for divine revelation of the proper pathway to follow during the present difficulties. David asks God to destroy the enemies for what they have done. Not only have they harmed the king but they have flouted God's moral law.

At this point in the psalm David tells of the joy that all who trust in the Lord will surely experience. Finally, assurance is given that the righteous will be protected (*shielded*). Among the important philosophic questions is whether people can have that kind of direct relationship with God. The question seems to be answered here with assurance.

Justice and Mercy (Psalm 6)

Serious physical, mental, and spiritual sickness is the complaint of the psalmist in this poem. The colorful imagery of troubled bones and a drenched couch intensifies the portrait of a dying person whom God has abandoned. A sense of total desperation pervades the first three of the psalm's four stanzas. In stanza one, the first words are a penitent plea of a sinner who hopes for relief from punishment inflicted in the form of this severe illness. The words are a cry for mercy, including the oft-quoted *O Lord, how long?*

The second stanza (verses 4-5) reveals the sinner's last faint hope for restoration of health. God's love is known to be steadfast; therefore, it is appropriate for the sinner to expect that deliverance will come. And for another reason God must save this sinner's life. Why? It is impossible for one to remember God after death or to offer praise from Sheol, the realm of the dead which God never visits.

Stanza three provides further description of the troubled person's physical circumstances, here with obvious hyperbole. More likely the outpouring of all that water is simply the psalmist's pillow wet with tears. Yet the emotional overstatements add dramatic emphases to the supplication. The reference to fading eyesight (verse 7) may be the typical effects of the aging process, perhaps cataracts.

The tone of the poem changes in the final stanza to one of unbreakable faith in God. Despite the deep grief, there is the calm sense of assurance that God will hear his prayer and drive the evildoers away. We assume that the physical and mental distress is being attributed by the psalmist to enemies—a different impression from the one the first verse seems to convey.

Let Justice Be Done (Psalm 7)

This psalm was probably written in David's time by a person hounded by enemies, apparently Benjaminites who were known to be allied with Saul. The style is somewhat irregular with stanzas of varying length. Throughout the poetry some remarkable legal history is developed around the theme of justice, both human and divine. Verses one and two are clearly an appeal for help. The simile *like a lion* points to the urgency of the situation which is doubtless violent. The quest for justice begins in verses 3-5. It is a well-reasoned argument for justice in the best tradition of the ancient Near East. Some knowledge of the Code of Hammurabi is evident in the suggestion (verse 5) that the enemy be permitted appropriate retribution if indeed the psalmist should be judged guilty. In stanza three there is a second appeal for judgment, restated as an impassioned plea to God to convene the divine company of heaven. Surely, then, the psalmist will be vindicated and his righteousness and integrity finally proved.

The fourth stanza (verses 9-12) is an act of praise recognizing God's own righteousness, the divine method of determining human guilt or innocence, and God's unfailing ability to provide salvation to the upright in heart. The last stanza describes what God does to evildoers and what happens to the wicked who have incurred divine wrath as a consequence of the verdict. This passage offers a remarkably accurate picture of middle eastern justice, particularly verse 16, where justice includes punishment using the same crime which the evildoer committed.

The song closes with an earnest vow of thanksgiving and praise, assuming that the verdict has been rendered in the psalmist's favor, that justice was served and just deserts meted out.

How Majestic Is Your Name (Psalm 8)

Here is a glorious hymn of Creation, clearly a poetic paraphrase of Genesis 1. It opens with words ascribing majesty to God's name throughout the universe. The word *name* had a connotation much broader than simply a title. It was, for Israel, the mighty presence of God revealed in the natural world. Appropriately, therefore, this psalm was sung at eventide when the glorious Middle-Eastern night sky was revealed by the advancing darkness.

Verse 2 reveals one of the more unique paradoxes of God's character. It is the appointment of lowly, weak, non-warlike personalities to the most monumental and world-shaking tasks. The babes and infants are, figuratively, just such persons. Moses and Jesus, born in poverty and laid in humble baskets and mangers, became the makers of civilization. It is they who *silence the enemy (NRSV) or foe* (NIV).

Verses 3-8 are a profound meditation about the nature of the humanity God has created. It begins with words of wonder about God's magnificent physical universe. The psalmist's solo monologue then turns to the crucial question of Psalms: *What is man* (NIV; NRSV = *human beings*) *that you are mindful of him?* And at once a flood of phrases provides an answer. God has given power to the people to dominate the world. How perceptive of the psalmist to recognize that dominion and power as evidence of God's grace by the addition of verse 9. It is a repetition of verse 1 and is fitting indeed. It symbolizes the humility that ought to characterize the acceptance of all the responsibility God has given to humanity. To have such a feeling would seem appropriate to today's people as well.

Evil Enemies (Psalm 9)

Biblical scholars are of the opinion that Psalms 9 and 10 were originally one longer psalm. The central theme of the two poems is the historic issue of why the wicked prosper and retain good health while the faithful adherents to God's moral precepts suffer both poverty and sickness. The problem is timeless in all of human history. It has not been (and doubtless never will be) completely resolved by political and social measures. In this psalm, some views of the issue are set forth; they may be helpful in dealing with economic disparity.

Psalm 9 is one of ritualistic preparation for the main theme to be elucidated in Psalm 10. The ritual begins with a beautiful prayer of thanksgiving and praise. It fairly rings with the simple joys of being alive. The reason for this happiness is revealed in verses 3 and 4. God has vindicated the psalmist, falsely accused by enemies who in turn have been rebuked by God's judgments. Verses 5-10 comprise a solemn proclamation of faith and trust that God will judge the pagan nations and, under universal sovereignty, govern all peoples with equity. Following this are two brief stanzas entreating the worshipers to sing praises to God who will not forget the poor, and offering a testimony that God did provide salvation in order that the psalmist might sing praises at the Temple gates.

As the ritual continues in verses 15-20, God's righteous judgment upon the wicked nations is reiterated, a petition for their ultimate destruction is offered, and a plea is made for the poor and the needy. At this juncture Psalm 9 is ended but the poem is continued in the next chapter.

Poverty and Suffering (Psalm 10)

The theological argument of this continuing liturgical drama begins in the opening lines with the question, *Why, O Lord, do you stand far off? Why do you hide yourself in times of trouble?* These plaintive cries are followed immediately by a long recitation (verses 2-9) about the prosperous, wicked people who never seem to suffer even though they persecute the poor and reject the universal sovereignty of God. The plight of the poor is told in verses 10-11 where abject despair is the dominant mood.

Finally, as if in desperation, the psalmist turns again to God, begging for divine intervention, and in verses 14-18 sings a prophetic oracle of faith that justice will be done. Thus the central issue, posed in Psalm 9, is triumphantly resolved.

§ § § § § § §

The Message of Psalms 1–10

Part One of the book of Psalms describes the most important questions with which religious people of the ancient Near East were confronted. The language of the individual psalms provides interesting insight into the cultural surroundings in which the authors lived as well as the social and political environment in which their religious faith was being developed and tested. Those questions and the answers which emerged seem hardly different from those of our contemporary civilization.

§ What are the characteristics of the righteous?

§ Does God's universal sovereignty apply to all nations, even the heathen?

§ Can the faithful person be confident that God will be a shield against danger?

§ Will God vindicate the falsely accused?

§ Will God relieve the repentant sinner from the distress of acute illness?

§ Can faithful people be assured of God's justice?

§ Will people be humble even when God has given them almost unlimited power over all the earth?

§ Why do the wicked prosper and flourish while the righteous suffer?

§ § § § § § §

PART TWO Psalms 11–20

Introduction to These Psalms

In this part of the book of Psalms, the titles give David credit as the author. His lovely poetry contains vivid word pictures of what God is really like. David's profound depths of faith made God a spiritual reality and that reality is never in doubt, even during the darkest hours of tragedy and despair.

The words in these poems are uttered with such simple and yet forceful conviction. Little wonder that many of the concepts expressed in this group of psalms have found their way into the most significant theological beliefs about the nature of God. Your study of this cluster of the Psalms will be helped by considering the way God chooses to make manifest the divine nature in the affairs of the nations and their people.

God's Law and Order (Psalm 11)

This psalm was evidently written during a time when political governments of the region had fallen into terrible disrepute. Law and order were absent from day-to-day affairs. So bad was it that even the Lord counseled the righteous to flee like birds to the mountains. Doubtless the mountains were seen as the safest refuge if the foundations of society (its principles of law and order) were being destroyed. As the psalm begins, the dreadful state of society is made plain (verses 1-3). The psalmist then turns with complete confidence to a word picture of God *in his holy temple.* There, in verse 4, the Lord is envisioned on a judgment seat entering the consciousness of all the nations' peoples with a severely critical stare. Much like a teacher with schoolchildren, God gazes relentlessly, testing the consciences of the people. In the process neither the righteous nor the wicked escape the energy of God's eyes emanating from under the arched eyebrows.

The Lord is further depicted (verse 5) as hating the ways of the violent on whom just punishment shall be visited. The metaphor of fire and brimstone is reminiscent of God's justice (and vengeance) dealt to Sodom and Gomorrah (Genesis 19:24). The *scorching wind* refers to the natural, regional disaster occurring on occasion as violent winds blow from the vast desert lands of northern Arabia westward toward Israel and the Mediterranean Sea.

The psalm closes with beautiful lines proclaiming God's concern for those whose lives are righteous and upright in heart and who live within the divine principles of law and order. They shall see the face of the Lord in due time.

God's Precious Words (Psalm 12)

Four stanzas of two verses each comprise this anthem revealing the purity and truth of God's words contrasted with those of lying, deceitful people. It is not in God's nature to be a flattering hypocrite.

The first stanza begins with a plea for help, followed by a clear assessment of what unfaithful people are doing. The *double heart* (NRSV; NIV= *deception*) is interesting poetic imagery for one who says one thing while thinking another.

In the second stanza the psalmist calls to God for just punishment on all deceitful braggarts and liars.

A subtle hint about the sin of pride may be read in verse 4 as it describes people who believe they can talk their way into ultimate control of their own destiny as well as that of others.

The third stanza is God's response, an oracle which

vows rescue and a haven of refuge for the victim. The
Lord's words are followed by the psalmist's assurance
that divine words can be trusted as if they were pure
silver. The metaphor comparing words to precious
metals alludes to the ancient process of refining ore in a
crucible, heating and cooling it seven times as each
successive treatment removes a bit more of the
impurities. The final stanza has two distinct parts: Verse
7 is a lovely one-sentence prayer for protection, while
verse 8 echoes the prevailing theme of appalling evil
among the nation's people.

God's Steadfast Love (Psalm 13)

Here is a remarkable affirmation that God listens to
people in distress. Clearly, among the numerous virtues
of our Lord, none can be quite so compelling as a
response to an anguished call for help. The setting for
this story could be anywhere at any time. It is humanity's
distress at its most poignant.

The poetic arrangement is slightly irregular, the first of
three stanzas consisting of four plaintive lines, each of
which begins with the desolate wail, *How long?* Think of
the wonderfully dramatic mood these words establish as
the psalmist is stating his case. Does God deliberately
forget? The mood is abject loneliness. Does God hide
from us? The mood is absolute rejection. Does God inflict
mental and spiritual distress? The mood is unbearable
anguish. Does God allow evil enemies to triumph? The
mood is utter hopelessness.

The *How long* soliloquy is followed by a stanza of two
verses (3-4) of earnest prayer for relief from enemies who
rejoice in their tyranny over victims. If God permits such
exultation, is trust possible at all? The final stanza is a
firm declaration that God is not at all what that dramatic
monologue portrayed. Quite to the contrary, God does
save the righteous out of the depths of unending,
trustworthy, and steadfast love. And because God has

redeemed the grieving psalmist and provided merciful relief from persecution, God is most worthy of thanksgiving and praise.

God Is! (Psalm 14)

Here the psalmist speaks to the prevailing attitude of godlessness among the nations. The subject is timeless, appropriate to all ages. To emphasize the point, David sings a line at the outset which is the pivotal point for the serious student of the philosophy of religion: Is there a God? How does one argue the question? Fools have said in their hearts, *"There is no God."*

Intellectual assault on the fool of this remarkable psalm has grown through the ages to a veritable mountain of volumes defending the premises and conclusions that a living God does exist. The more curious among students of the Bible will find great fascination in delving into the literature on this subject. We do not wish to discredit thoughtful, even crucial philosophic inquiry by moving too quickly to the psalmist's views. Yet David's proclamation is swift and certain. That God exists is implied at once (verse 2).

The Lord has often looked down from heaven. It may be that David is remembering Israel's history and the situations in which God intervened. The Flood and the destruction of Sodom are examples.

In verses 2-3, God is pictured as looking down and finding nothing but corruption, disloyalty, and utter wickedness. Is it time for another mighty act of cleansing? Yet in the next stanza, the psalmist seems to be drawing some distinctions between all the wicked of the preceding verses and those who were identified in verse 5 as the generations of the righteous. There is hope for those who remain faithful. The psalm closes with an exquisitely worded prayer invoking precious memories of a glorious past when the people of Jacob's (Israel's) God enjoyed good fortune. Oh, that it might be that way again!

The Presence of God (Psalm 15)

The principal question about the reality of God which this brief poem addresses is whether one can actually come near to the divine presence. Throughout the psalms there persists the clear and decisive idea that God is a God of personal communication. While a specific place for communication such as the sanctuary on Mount Zion may have been intended in this and other psalms, we believe that God does not have such limitations. Mystic omnipresence is an important theological principle. Once David has raised the possibility of entering into God's presence, the answer is proposed. It is phrased in verses 2-5 as teaching. Those who are allowed into God's presence are the righteous ones. The criteria are strict indeed. Taken literally, the requirements would be impossible for a less than perfect human being ever to meet. Therefore, these should be read and interpreted with both the ideals and the realities in mind. A composite picture might be drawn for a person who can closely approximate the ideal, at least by intention.

The concluding statement simply affirms that persons who are intent on living within the boundaries of these precepts will remain among the community of the righteous and regular inhabitants of the divine presence.

God's Presence Is Joy (Psalm 16)

The major concepts embodied in this psalm are generally the things that God can and will do to assist in periods of fear and distress. It is understood that God will preserve the psalmist. A solemn profession of faith has put a blessing on this agreement. The pact is further assured as, in verse 3, David places himself in the company of the saints—presumably noble persons in Israel's history who have earned favor with God.

Verse 4 is probably an antiphonal stanza conveying a picture of those who worship pagan gods and whose ritual requires the shedding and drinking of sacrificial blood. The names which David does not speak are those of the pagan gods not worthy of the same homage given to the God of Israel.

The chosen *portion* (verse 5) suggests a principle of faith: Everything belongs to the Lord.
The boundaries of the land on which David lives delineate good ground, an indication that God allots the earthly heritage to the faithful people, divine generosity having occurred.

In verse 7, David tells of God's counsel during the long hours of the night. This may be a reference to dreams or perhaps to contemplation during moments of sleeplessness in quiet darkness. Because his thoughts are continually turned toward God, those divine sources of strength and confidence are always available. This blissful state of mind and spirit creates a mood of constant joy and a feeling of security and safety. He knows with certainty that the desolation of death in Sheol or the fateful descent into the pit will not happen.

The psalm ends with a vigorous affirmation of the good life associated with God's wonderful counsel and joyous presence. Life with the Lord brings nothing but pleasure.

God Hears People (Psalm 17)

In this psalm, the predominant theme is assurance that God will be reliable and prompt in the administration of justice. The setting is an ancient courtroom. Sincerity and honesty are clearly evident as the psalmist enters a personal plea for justice. God is called upon to test the heart of the plaintiff who assures the court that no evil will be found. As the trial continues, the court hears (in verses 4-5) additional strains of innocence as unwavering perseverance in the way of the Lord is avowed. Worthy of note is the fact that the psalmist chooses not to introduce, for purposes of making comparisons, the wickedness of others. Rather, the pure, undefiled servant of God stands on that merit alone.

At this point (verses 6-14) the psalmist sings a prayer. It opens with a call to God with complete confidence, persuaded through experience, that God will respond because of the divine property of steadfast love. To be kept as the *apple* of your eye is to be among those whom God favors most of all. The plaintiff in this case cannot be content with simple supplication. It seems that God must be reminded that there are enemies who seek to destroy this righteous person. Those enemies are the subject of verses 9-12 which describe both their activities and their nature as ravenous lions. The lion was a symbol of violence in biblical times. Quite clearly the psalmist is in mortal fear of his life. His prayer closes with a ringing call for deliverance, followed by a puzzling wish that some persons among his enemies continue to prosper. Translators have been troubled by these lines, which may be incomplete. A possible solution is to assume that the psalmist has turned from a condemnation of the enemy to a petition for favorable treatment of members of the community of the righteous.

The final line of the psalm (verse 15) is a studied, introspective summation (appropriate to a trial) of feelings that have resulted from the trial and from faith in a God whose justice is unblemished. There is implicit in this conclusion that God will deliver vengeance upon the enemy and vindication to this righteous psalmist and that action will be taken by God before the first glimmer of the morning light of the following day. And with this strong assertion, the psalmist closes his case.

God's King Triumphs (Psalm 18)

The lines of this poem appear also in 2 Samuel 22:2-51. David is near the end of his reign and is reflecting on events during his kingship. He speaks of the unique powers of God who rescued him from peril again and again and strengthened him in his roles of warrior and king. For David the reality of God is absolutely assured.

And to substantiate the fact he sings about the power of God to rescue, about the God who commands the forces of nature, and about the God who sustains him in battle.

David begins this anthem with a stanza of praise which includes very familiar words describing God: *rock, fortress,* and *shield* (NIV) or *deliverer* (NRSV). The uncommon *horn of salvation* may be a reference to a bull's horn, perhaps a weapon. The second stanza (verses 4-6) relates perilous circumstances, the king's appeal for help, and the promise that God is listening.

That God is very much a part of David's life is evident from the powerful responses described in verses 7-15. The imagery reveals nature at its most tumultuous: earthquakes, volcanos, thunderstorms, and perhaps even eclipses. The *cherub* is a mythological representation of the wind. Exposing the valleys or the channels of the sea suggests cyclonic, tidal violence. But it may also remind the listeners that God does intervene in their lives, as was done at the Red Sea.

The aftermath of the display of natural power is not a devastated earth but a merciful act of personal salvation.

Verses 16-19 relate the role of God as the king's strong deliverer from calamitous circumstances. David sings of the wonderful things God has done for him. Verses 20-27 offer convincing testimony that God's loyalty is unfailing to those who are loyal in return, struggling to live lives of righteousness. David's personal recollections (verses 28-29) include some unusual things that God has done for him. His lamp was lit—a lovely figure of speech suggesting that direction was given to his life with vigor and zest added. Crushing a troop and leaping a wall allude to the gift of extraordinary physical strength.

Verses 31-39 are David's song of praise giving to God alone all praise and thanks for the support given to him in the execution of his monarchical duties. God made him swift as a deer (hind), gave him strength to bend the bronze bow (a metal weapon using energy like that of a heavy, coiled spring), and provided him with a shield of salvation—a metaphor for a mystic shroud which deflects all of the enemies' ammunition.

As the anthem draws to its conclusion, David continues his praise of God for mighty acts which have allowed the enemy (probably Saul) to be completely subdued. The final stanza is a stirring tribute to God, punctuated by promises to praise the name of God to all the world, and by words of thanksgiving for victory and for the gift of love to David and his lineage—a promise fulfilled beyond measure a thousand years later in Bethlehem of Judea.

God's Universal Law (Psalm 19)

This psalm is a magnificent hymn of Creation. It deals not just with earth as a place for human habitation, but with the whole of the known universe. The poetry also tells of the founding of moral law as God's creative act of perfection. The psalm concludes with an appeal for an upright life and a very familiar prayer sentence.

The first section of this anthem was the inspiration for Haydn's stirring *Creation* oratorio, words of which have been translated into the English of a familiar hymn, *The Heavens Are Telling.* In these first two stanzas (verses 1-6), God makes a personal investment of handiwork and speech which create the physical universe and the laws of nature by which the universe is regulated. They are God's universal laws and, as verses 3-4 suggest, they remain unintelligible to the human ear and mind despite their universal applicability. Verses 4-6 are a picturesque view of the sky as a tent for the sun and the full range of its daily travels. The language has mythological associations as well as figures of speech which link human behavior to the natural world.

The second section of this hymn to God's majesty tells of a second magnificent creation, the laws by which the social and political universe of humanity is regulated.

This is, of course, moral law. It is not surprising that David should grasp the relevance of these two mighty creative acts and link them together in one anthem. He does not presume to offer specific detail about the moral law; that is left to the centuries of human experience to develop. What David does maintain are the purity, accuracy, and universality and eternal quality of the laws, commandments, and precepts of the Lord. Their precious value is extolled by a comparison to gold; their importance to human interaction is sweeter than honey.

The final segment of David's joyous proclamation of faith is a promise that he will henceforth maintain a respectful attitude toward God, keeping himself free from errors and faults (verse 12).

Perhaps the most profound insight into human frailty is David's prayer to be kept free from the sin of presumption. How easy it is to become a self-appointed voice of God, particularly as we attempt to interpret God's universe and laws as though we were speaking for all time. Verse 14 is a familiar benediction.

The reader will find it especially interesting to study this psalm in several of the available translations.

God Helps People (Psalm 20)

The anointed king enjoys God's special protection. This characteristic of the God of Jacob is implied throughout the several stanzas. It assures the king that victory in an upcoming battle is inevitable. His enemies will collapse.

The first stanza of five verses appears to be a congregational chant, beseeching God's help for the king. The name of God is not to be understood as a magic emblem but as a pervasive, intimate presence during the king's undertakings. Verse 6 is the opening line of the king's solo. David promises victory to the congregation, especially because he will be assisted by the Lord. He makes the claim that God's name is more effective in battle than great numbers of horses and chariots. The concept is fundamental to David's faith. He again pledges to the people that he will be victorious and the enemy will be vanquished. In the final stanza (verse 9), the congregation responds with a plea to God for victory.

§ § § § § § §

The Message of Psalms 11–20

The general theme in this part is the nature of God. These ten psalms contain a noteworthy collection of lustrous ideas about Israel's God and what the people and the king thought their God was like. David had unfailing faith and was very secure in his belief that he knew the living God. He relates these convictions in ways that show how the character of God was revealed to him again and again.

§ God is a good listener.

§ God is always at the side of Israel's king; this enables him to be triumphant.

§ God creates and sustains the universe. The creation includes humanity which is given special dominion over the creatures of God's natural world.

§ God is the author of the principles of law and order by which society is governed.

§ God is love and that love is steadfast, abiding forever against all onslaughts.

§ Even though fools may believe there is no God, faithful people know that God exists.

§ God's presence is something that people can feel when they are near to it.

§ There is joy just being in that presence.

§ God is especially attentive to persons who have been given a divine mandate to rule.

§ § § § § § §

Psalms 21–31

Introduction to These Psalms

The Psalms are sources of comfort and help in our dealings with difficult and trying circumstances. But they are also appropriate for periods of quiet contemplation when personal affinity with God is the heart's desire. The great value in moments of untroubled meditation is the opportunity to cultivate a serene and spiritual life-style.

Most of the psalms in this group of eleven lend themselves quite well to thoughtful study of ways to live confidently in the security of God's steadfast love. The Twenty-third Psalm is exemplary. It is the principal psalm of confidence and comfort. Other psalms in this group will also be helpful as one grapples with situations of illness, injustice, and false accusations as well as tribulations of spiritual and mental anguish. Reading Psalm 21, we can rejoice with the king, visualizing the righteous among us in positions of leadership to be the calm and confident beloved of God.

Prayers for the King (Psalm 21)

Here is a joyous hymn sung as a prayer for the king. It might also be fit for thoughtful contemplation about the life and times of any person in a position of leadership. Three segments comprise the psalm. In verses 1-7, the congregation voices thanks for the good things God has done for the king (David, evidently). The first two verses introduce the general theme of rich blessings. The king's loyalty to God is then proclaimed. There follows an inventory of blessings: crown of gold (a symbol of riches), a long life, a glorious reign, and supreme joy in the presence of God. Verse 7 is a congregational refrain echoing the assurance of the king's loyalty and trust.

The second section of the hymn (verses 8-12) is the congregational restatement of the king's most frequently cited difficulty. He is constantly beset by enemies and he worries passionately about them. Here the hymn involves both God and the king in the struggle. It is clearly no simple set-to with neighboring tribes; the psalmist in verse 10 is anticipating a cataclysm in which all enemies will be completely destroyed. The blazing oven suggests the image of an entire community on fire.

The third section of the hymn is a two-line oracle challenging the king to live up to God's expectations of him, praising the splendid blessings of great mental and physical stamina.

Yet Will I Believe (Psalm 22)

This long poem has traditionally been read at Good Friday services. The first line, the fourth of the Seven Last Words of Christ on the cross, suggests why. Elsewhere within the first section of this psalm (verses 1-21), other phrases are vivid reminders of events leading up to the crucifixion. For this reason the psalm has been interpreted by some as prophetic of the passion and death of Jesus.

The psalm opens with four stanzas arranged antiphonally, the first being the agonized call for help, the second (verses 3-5) a testimony of praise and trust. In the third stanza the psalmist resumes the lament which has all the characteristics of the days following Palm Sunday. In stanza four, we read a prayer of thanks and a plea for assistance.

A second array of four stanzas completes the first section. Here a picture of total deterioration is painted;

the finality of ~~death~~ is certain. The bulls (verse 12) are probably wild oxen or bison from the grasslands of Bashan, a region east of the Sea of Galilee. Verses 14-15 depict a state of complete physical degeneration. The words are spoken with a sense of utter hopelessness and futility. In the following stanza, the psalmist's condition seems to be even worse. Wild dogs (hyenas, perhaps) have now begun an attack. The imagery of pierced feet and hands suggests intense pain. ~~Death~~ cannot be too far off now; the psalmist watches hopelessly as enemies gamble for his clothing. The final verses (19-21) of the first section are an earnest prayer for deliverance.

Some dispute exists among scholars as to whether the second section (verses 22-31) is actually a separate psalm. The argument in favor of the single-psalm theory is quite compelling, especially if one agrees that God did answer the earnest prayer for deliverance. That being so, the remainder of the psalm is a glorious hymn of praise and thanksgiving. What makes this story so appealing is that the psalmist is thinking not just of himself but of other people as well. The hope is that people who have been similarly afflicted shall also be healed. In what may be understood as a broad and most unselfish outlook on the whole world, the psalmist prays that all the nations of the world and generations not yet born shall become the people of God and be delivered from all adversity.

The Lord Is My Shepherd (Psalm 23)

None of the psalms is more beloved than this one. From the earliest religious experiences of childhood (memorizing Bible verses among them) to the hearing of elegies during Christian ~~burial~~ the Twenty-third Psalm is there. Reasons for its attractiveness are not hard to find. One is its graceful simplicity. Few poems say so much in so few words. Other reasons appear in the train of thought as the poetry progresses.

To say and think, *The Lord is my shepherd,* is to establish personal, intimate affinity with God. It is to enter a right relationship, the advantages of which are feelings of perfect peace and contentment and of not being in need of or in want for anything. Lying down in green pastures and walking beside still waters are lovely word pictures, representing the actions of sheep in the presence of the good shepherd who cares very deeply. This is the God to whom we have entrusted ourselves and who provides peaceful nights and uncluttered days, despite the difficulties which life holds. It is the same God who nurtures the renewal of life, especially the inner personality. When the soul is restored, we are not just refurbished for the day's work. We are renewed in the deepest recesses of the mind and spirit and open completely to the closest association with the mind of God.

The intimate presence of the living God is further dramatized as the shepherd (verse 3) is given the role of counselor and teacher, leading the sheep along the right pathway. And the shepherd does this for *his name's sake,* which seems to say that this is done so that others may know of the good things happening when relations are right between the shepherd and the sheep.

In verse 4, the psalmist dwells further on the shepherd's care; this time it is watchfulness when the sheep are in peril. The shepherd, using the tools of his trade (rod and staff), protects the sheep from deadly perils lurking along the edges of steep, rocky ravines lining the grazing lands. The imagery is wonderfully tender. The psalmist has had a brush with death—an accident or illness perhaps. But the good shepherd has kept him from the valley of shadows.

In the last stanza (verses 5-6) the shepherd is now the host, preparing a banquet. But an odd circumstance prevails. The psalmist must sit down to dine with enemies! In numerous other psalms, enemies are to be feared, distrusted, and often violently dealt with. But here God (the host) is bringing opponents together. Reconciling foes is one more evidence of grace.

In the tradition of the times, a guest was anointed with aromatic oils (verse 5) and the drinking cup was continuously filled to overflowing. That word picture is one of contentment and peace. The psalmist is so filled with the joyous presence of God that he knows that all the days ahead shall be as idyllic as this one.

The King of Glory (Psalm 24)

This beautiful poem, subject of modern hymns and great choral music, proclaims that temple gates shall lift their heads as the King of Glory enters the sanctuary. This powerful metaphor of ancient doors responding as if they were persons is the climax of the psalm. It is preceded by a declaration of God's universal mastery of the earth and its waters and by a ritual of inquiry to determine who is worthy to enter into the presence of the Lord.

This dramatic episode is in three parts. Verses 1 and 2 are hymnic lines praising God who has fashioned the inhabitable earth by planting it firmly in the waters which by divine power have been brought under control. The short hymn is followed by a question-and-answer litany of two verses. A priest seeks to discover the qualities of persons who may enter the sanctuary; a second priest responds with the familiar clean hands and pure hearts. Words of assurance follow, saying that all persons will be rewarded with God's blessing.

The final, climactic stanza is sung antiphonally by choristers. First is the petition to make ready the temple gates that the King of Glory (God) may enter. The response asks for some information about the King. The response further depicts him as a victorious God of battle. Then the petition to open the gates is repeated and the final response asks again who the King of Glory is. It is followed by the emphatic answer, *The LORD of hosts* (NRSV) or *Almighty* (NIV). This psalm might well be on our lips as we enter the church and sit quietly in those moments before the service, there to sense the presence of the King of Glory.

Teach Me, O Lord (Psalm 25)

The structure of this psalm is somewhat irregular. It contains several stanzas of differing lengths, the first of which (verses 1-7) is a prayer for good counsel and personal security. The psalmist evidently has guilt feelings about sins of the past. Thus, the prayer takes on the character of hungering deeply for an intimate, forgiving relationship with God. Hoping for the achievement of such a blissful state, the psalmist declares complete trust in God (verses 8-14) as teacher and leader. The mood here seems to be one of increasing confidence in God's faithfulness. The psalmist sings of the certainty that God will maintain the covenant, and in so doing will keep the psalmist prosperous and safe from life's most vexing predicaments (the *net* (NRSV) or *snare* (NIV) of verse 15).

Following these stanzas of praise the poetry turns to a prayer, revealing a human being in affliction and deep distress, pleading once again for forgiveness and the serenity which comes from God's protection. The psalmist waits for the Lord and is led from personal concerns to thoughts of Israel and the national need for redemption.

Test Me, O Lord (Psalm 26)

This psalm is an invigorating song of a person with complete confidence in the relationship with God. It is not a song for persons who are self-righteous, arrogant, and boastful about their own virtues. If we assume David to be the author, the psalm must have been written at a time when his confidence and trust in God were complete and assured without question. It is David's song proclaiming his love of God and his intense pleasure at being in God's house. Moreover, it is simply a song which expresses delight at the prospect of having this intimate personal alliance with the living God. For David, there is no other to whom he would extend such loyalty and no other to whom he could ever be so devoted. In one sense, the verses of the psalm are a recital of his reactions as he has tried to rule judiciously in concert with his Lord.

David's dealings have been accomplished with integrity and in accord with faithfulness to God's precepts (verses 1-3). He has not consorted with liars and agitators, nor has he had anything to do with wicked people (verses 4-5). His life has been entirely one of devotion to and adoration of God (verses 6-7). Moreover, he has looked forward with enthusiasm to being in the presence of God (verse 8) in the Temple. David's hope is to be spared the need to associate with sinners, gamblers, and reprobates (verses 9-10).

In the last stanza (verses 11-12), David affirms his own devotion to a life of righteousness. What a wonderful feeling of comfort, confidence, and serenity there is in living a life of trust in God's steadfast love.

A Courtroom Drama (Psalm 27)

Two distinct poems comprise this psalm: The first is a song of confidence (verses 1-6); the second is an agonized lament (verses 7-14). In both poems, the psalmist is evidently on trial. One might imagine the psalm to be a drama in two acts. Act one opens with a stirring declaration of trust by the central figure, an innocent person falsely accused of some crime. The Lord is described (verse 1) in familiar language: *light, salvation,* and *stronghold.* As the drama unfolds, the psalmist claims (verse 2) that the accusers will be the ones to suffer when their false charges are not sustained. To emphasize the point that the accused will be found innocent, the psalmist invokes some colorful imagery: Imagine that although great armies are warring against me, even so I am confident of being vindicated.

In verse 4 a softer approach is taken. The psalmist relates his deep yearnings for constant companionship with the Lord. The good life is to live in the Lord's house, to see the Lord face to face, and to be able to inquire after knowledge. This scene should not be interpreted to mean life after life. What the psalmist is seeking is the sweet experience of God, now.

In verse 5 the drama continues as the psalmist further declares his trust. The words suggest remembrance of stories of the early wanderings of Israel. God's *tent* (NRSV) or *tabernacle* (NIV) was a place of refuge and worship. The climax of act one is the clear statement of vindication followed by the promise to perform the rituals with a joyful heart and to participate regularly in the music of praise to the God who is the deliverer. Act two is much more somber, though it does end with optimistic hope. It begins with a cry for help. One can imagine the sobbing and wailing of this tortured victim from whom God seems to have turned away. Not even the parents (verse 10) have any further interest. The lament is punctuated by some words of confidence that perhaps the Lord has not forsaken the psalmist altogether. With words of earnest supplication, the victim pleads for protection and, in the face of the direst straits, poignantly affirms the belief (verse 13) that God will be revealed before death closes in. Verse 14 appears to be the advice of a priest of the Temple who has participated in the trial and has been persuaded of the psalmist's innocence.

The Lord Is a Refuge (Psalm 28)

The psalm is written for a person who is desperately ill. This is apparent from the language of the first stanza. It begins with a cry for help addressed to the Lord, the *rock*, a symbol of stability. The psalmist fears that death will occur if the Lord does not hear. ~~Death~~ in this case means going down to the *Pit*, the land of silence (Sheol), where God never goes. As the pleading continues, the hands are raised, a common gesture that signals human desperation.

The second stanza is the psalmist's petition to be spared from all association with wicked hypocrites. A curse on the enemies is spoken here along with a request that God should give them their just deserts. Why? They do not care about God so why shouldn't they be destroyed?

In the third stanza (verses 6-7), an oracle for healing is offered, presumably by one of the Temple singers. It ends with words of thanksgiving on the assumption that health and strength are to be regained. The final stanza includes two verses, one being poetry praising God's loving care of the anointed king and the people. The other is a petition for salvation for the people now and for generations yet to come. It is expected that, because those future generations are God's heritage, they will be cared for forever as the good shepherd cares for the sheep.

The Voice of Thunder (Psalm 29)

This psalm is one of the great nature poems. It is of ancient origin, apparently an adaptation of a mythological Canaanite story of a weather god. Like Psalms 8 and 9, this hymn depicts God as controller of natural forces. Because the storms are under divine control, the people of God attain security and confidence despite the potential for devastation.

The story is in three sections, beginning with a call to praise. It is addressed to heavenly beings, lesser gods perhaps, who are expected to give homage to God in the beauty of holiness. Section two (verses 3-9) is a sevenfold litany in which God speaks seven times as the voice of thunder. The poetry is beautiful, colorful imagery of the destructive power of thunderstorms which sweep over Palestine from Sirion (Mount Hermon) in the north to the deserts (Kadesh) in the south. The storm topples the giant cedars of Lebanon and literally shakes the mountains as if they are terrified young animals. Lightning flashes and winds strong enough to strip leaves from the trees are further elements of the raging storm. Through it all, God controls the resulting floods.

The final section is the glorification and enthronement of God as king forever. The psalm closes with petitions for strength and peace.

The Lord Is Gracious (Psalm 30)

This psalm is a lovely hymn of praise to a gracious God who redeemed the king. David was in deep distress, beset again by enemies and physically ill. His gratitude seems boundless for God has saved him from the depths of eternal darkness (Sheol). While the latter condition may be somewhat exaggerated, David is so exuberant about feeling good that he cannot help summoning the congregation to share his joy. In a brief moment of reflection, David tells the people that while God shows anger from time to time, it is momentary and fleeting. This characteristic of God is likened to sorrow and weeping in the evening when one may be out of favor with God and to joy in the morning when the tribulation caused by divine anger has dissipated and serenity returns.

David's wisdom is manifested again in verses 6-7 where he describes himself as self-righteously prosperous. He has become like the king of the mountain, the master of his fate and the captain of his soul. Then, in the absence of humility, David is brought again to the edge of the Pit, from where he is forced to cry anew for help for redemption from certain death.

The utter graciousness of God is told in the final stanza as David, once more, is favored. The declaration that his gratitude is forever ends this great hymn of confidence in the limitless reservoirs of God's grace.

My Times Are in Your Hand (Psalm 31)

Some scholars have suggested that this poem ought to be two psalms. Presently it may be treated as poetic drama with two independent scenes. The first is about a person besieged by enemies and falsely accused, the second about one who is terribly ill and wasting away. The two scenes may form a coherent unity as, in the end, both persons enjoy salvation.

A rather familiar (by now) opening line is the confession of faith in which God is a refuge, fortress, or rock. The petition for speedy assistance which follows asks God to spare the psalmist from the net. This suggests entangling perils and traps set by the enemies. But the psalmist is not dismayed; a commitment has been made (verse 5). Recall that Jesus quoted this line, the seventh and last word on the cross. Verses 6-8 are words of appreciation for salvation, for being set in a broad place where enemies cannot lurk.

The second scene begins with verse 9. A picture of complete despair and desolation is painted. Totally outcast and forgotten, the psalmist cries as if the words were coming from deep in Sheol. This is doubtless the grimmest scene anywhere in the psalms. God's curse has been spoken. The metaphor of a broken, shattered clay pot surely means the absolute end.

Then suddenly God intervenes and the psalmist is restored and renewed. Confidence is reaffirmed by the loveliest of sentences, *My times are in your hands* (verse 15).

Once the restoration is complete, the psalmist sings a hymn of four stanzas. It begins with a petition for deliverance from enemies. They are the plotters and schemers who should be dispatched to death. The second stanza (verses 19-20) praises God's goodness and thanks God for keeping the faithful safe from malicious slander. Stanza three of this hymn is a personal blessing of God by the psalmist. The hymn comes to an end with a priestly oracle that seems to summarize what has gone before, that one may be of good courage when *my times are in your hands.*

§ § § § § § §

The Message of Psalms 21–31

This part of the Psalms emphasizes a point made earlier in part two that God is entirely trustworthy. Writers and recorders of these psalms stress the confidence we can all have in God's reliability. From this assurance we gain convictions, taking comfort that we can live life serenely.

§ A righteous king of Israel is favored by the Lord.

§ In the midst of serious affliction, a faithful person will still trust in God.

§ God heals the afflicted.

§ We can be serene and confident knowing that the Lord is our shepherd.

§ Who is the king of glory? God is the King of glory!

§ Who may enter the sanctuary? Those whose hands are clean and whose hearts are pure.

§ Being in God's loving and forgiving presence is among life's greatest pleasures.

§ God participates in the human effort to secure justice.

§ The psalmist's portrayal of death is being sent to Sheol, a land where God never goes.

§ God speaks to the nations by means of the forces of nature, thunderstorms being especially dramatic.

§ God may appear to be angry at times but that anger is only temporary.

§ To feel that one's life and times are in God's hands is to capture the essence of perfect serenity.

§ § § § § § §

Psalms 32– 41

Introduction to These Psalms

Among the important human rights elaborated in the American Declaration of Independence is the pursuit of happiness. This right was equally important to Israel when this magnificent collection of poems was being created. Part Four of the Psalms deals generally with the state of being happy. While God had not promised a continuous condition of bliss or life forever in the Garden of Eden, Israel understood that the covenant did not preclude enjoying life, free from anguish and suffering. But, as the world has discovered, and so did the people of Israel, true happiness is not the same as pleasure and bliss.

Happiness or blessedness is reflected differently in these lines. Psalm 32 opens with a beatitude. What could make people any happier than to know that their sins are forgiven?

Freedom from Guilt (Psalm 32)

The psalm opens with the psalmist's vigorous expression of joy and thanksgiving. God has removed the pain of guilt. Blame has been taken away and the soul is cleansed. While no specific sins are described, it is clear that estrangement from God is complete. Among the more difficult problems with which the psalmist had been forced to deal was the stubborn refusal to acknowledge the personal condition of sin. How easy it is to deceive one's self. Yet somehow, with God's help, this courageous person found the will to repent and to confess (verse 5) and so found blessed redemption.

The psalmist then turns to God and declares, in a prayer of two beautiful lines, a feeling of complete trust and confidence. What more blissful state than to be beyond the reach of all harm? Because of the happiness the psalmist has achieved, there is an eagerness to share this blessed experience. So an oracle is delivered (verses 8-11). It comes from a heart that is experienced in the way of sin and, having received salvation, now knows the way of God's moral precepts.

The admonition to avoid being both headstrong and stubborn is cleverly pictured by the use of horse and mule. And then with the literary device of antithesis (verse 10), in clear and simple terms, the two ways of life are contrasted. The final verse is a joyous call to rejoice in the praise of God.

Secure in the Lord (Psalm 33)

This psalm is liturgical, written to create a mood of worship in the sanctuary. It begins with a stirring call to rejoice and to praise God with instrumental music and singing (verses 1-3). The remainder of the text, except the final stanza, contains an abundance of reasons for this exuberant praise. Their enumeration begins in the second stanza with what God does (fills the earth with love) and what God is (a lover of justice). Verse 4 implies that God's work is done by the power of the *word*. It is an important theological concept in the New Testament, decisive in the Gospel of John.

Reasons for praise in the third stanza (verses 6-9) are God's creation and control of the universe. These lines are followed by a parallel stanza, God's control of the political world. It is an affirmation of the concept of universal sovereignty, but it is also prophetic as the psalmist sings the beatitude for the nation of Israel, which God has chosen.

Verses 13-19 provide additional reasons for praise, among them God's creative power in fashioning the hearts (spirits) of the nation's people and caring for them in ways that preclude the necessity of relying entirely on military power. Verses 18-19 add a warm, human touch as God is praised for keeping a watchful eye on those who hope.

The final stanza is a prayerful congregational response, the people waiting confidently, hopefully, and humbly for God's self-revelation.

The Good Life (Psalm 34)

The historical origin of this psalm is found in 1 Samuel 21:10-15, where David feigned insanity in order to escape from the Philistine king. The opening stanza of the psalm is David's grateful thanks for deliverance. In giving thanks he offers all the credit to God, taking no personal glory nor boasting in himself. The second stanza (verses 4-10) is David's tale of what happened to him and how he was saved. It includes an admonition that fear of the Lord is the best way to experience goodness. The *saints* (NIV) of verse 9 are the ordinary people of this world who are God's *holy ones* (NRSV). The young *lions* (verse 10) are fractious, rambunctious unbelievers.

In the third stanza David takes the role of teacher of the young and asks them how they would achieve happiness. The answer follows and is given in words of admonition in verses 13-14.

David then turns to a meditation (verses 15-21) on the nature of justice. The eyes and ears of verse 15 are figures of speech for a just God's vigilance in support of the faithful. The face of the Lord means the presence, the author of divine retribution, a critical feature of Hebrew belief. It is clear from David's discussion that the righteous are not immune from distress, but if one's attitude is rightly attuned to divine moral precepts God will help.

The final verse summarizes the poem. While God is the redeemer of those who believe, this does not indicate ~~eternal life,~~ a concept not often found in the Psalms. The heart of the matter is that righteous people are not going to be condemned to Sheol, the ~~silent land~~ of the ~~dead.~~

Delight in Salvation (Psalm 35)

In this long psalm David is in court pleading for the kind of happiness which will follow from a verdict of *not guilty*. In this instance he is on trial before the Lord. David has been pursued, hounded, trapped in a net, and is about to fall into a pit dug for the capture of wild animals. While these troubles may be exaggerations, the purpose is to convince the court that God has abandoned him. Yet he is hopeful that God will argue in his behalf at the trial (verses 1-3).

As the trial begins, a petition is offered for the enemies' destruction by a militant angel. An intermission then occurs in the proceedings. David breaks into a joyous song of praise in anticipation of a judgment favorable to him. Following this is a second plea for deliverance (verses 11-16), this one delivered to the court by poetic oratory of some intensity and vehemence. The decision to enter the court in sackcloth was made to create a dramatic effect.

David then turns, momentarily, to address a question to God along with words of praise (verses 17-18). But, overcome by the emotional climate of the courtroom, he again launches an intense argument, praying earnestly for the defeat of godless enemies.

David's final summation is a masterpiece of ritual poetry. He summons God to join the cause of righteousness in his case, condemns the enemy once more (verse 26), and invites those who believe in his innocence to shout with him in continuous and joyous praise to God who has, happily, given him salvation.

Excellent Lovingkindness (Psalm 36)

Here is a lovely meditation in three parts about God's faithfulness to the righteous and the sad plight of the godless. Verses 1-4 are an oracle on the state of sinfulness using a personified evil spirit, possibly a demon to be exorcised. The wicked person has rejected wisdom and seems committed to crimes which are plotted during sleepless nights. Interestingly, the wicked are not in fear of God's judgment; the very idea of God does not have meaning for deliberately sinful people.

In part two (verses 5-9), the psalmist contemplates God's unfailing love. The vastness of God's faithfulness to the people of Israel is beyond measure. It is picturesquely compared to the unfathomable heights of mountains and depths of the seas. The precious nature of that divine love is beautifully depicted by word pictures: *shadow of your wings, abundance of your house, river of delights,* and *fountain of life.* Could true happiness be better fulfilled?

The final part of the psalm is a prayer for assurance that God's love will permeate the lives of the faithful. In verses 11-12 the psalmist prays for protection and for the subjugation of the wicked.

The Heart's Desire (Psalm 37)

This psalm is a lengthy, somewhat repetitious poem reflecting the lessons taught by the nation's teachers of wisdom. The lessons are proverbial in form and deal with a variety of subjects generally related to God's moral law. True happiness, the heart's desire, is to be achieved when the admonitions are heeded and life is in tune with God's ethical precepts. This is one of few psalms addressed to the people and not to God.

A central theme seems to emerge in consideration of the conflict between good and evil. The righteous may be victimized for a time by the world's turmoil, but eventually they will be prosperous and happy. It is quite the other way around for the wicked. Terms used throughout to designate the righteous are interesting: *meek, poor, needy, upright* and *blameless*. They are further designated as *saints*—generous, wise, and obedient to the law.

Do not fret is a repeated admonition. It seems to suggest here that one ought never to worry nor allow oneself to envy the prosperity of the ungodly. Just deserts and punishment await them. Trust in God is the true basis of happiness. The psalm does not attempt to solve the crucial philosophic riddle of why the wicked prosper and the righteous suffer. It does suggest that ultimate peace and joy are to be in God's presence through faith. In this sense the poetry is prophetic of the New Testament.

The Price of Suffering (Psalm 38)

Doubtless this is not a song of happiness, although the biblical title indicates that it may have been used simply to evoke memories of severe distress and suffering in the past. The final stanza (verses 21-22) offers insight into a crucial element in the Israelite tradition, namely that hope is paramount in the conquest of even the deepest despair.

The central theme of this poem is that suffering is punishment for sin. The severity of the illness, presumably Hansen's disease (leprosy), is proof of the psalmist's evil condition and is surely evidence of God's anger. The picture of suffering is made all the more dramatic by the behavior of relatives and persons who once were friends, as well as enemies bent on murder (see verses 11-12).

At this point (verses 13-18) the psalmist is in the depths of despair. And from these depths we hear a cry for mercy and a confession of sin. The final act in the drama is a firm declaration of loyalty to God buoyed by hope for salvation.

Uncommon Despair (Psalm 39)

David is deeply involved here in the theological dilemma known as *theodicy*, the riddle of why there is human suffering in a universe created and controlled by a loving God. It is clear that a life of godliness does not relieve one of suffering. Some would believe, therefore, that the struggle to live righteously is an exercise in futility.

The riddle is not solved in this psalm, but some interesting insight is provided. In stanza one, David utters a determination not to talk about his distress for fear of offending God. But eventually his suffering grows so intense that he breaks the silence. His anguished cry to God in stanza two is simply to find out how long he can expect to live, knowing that human life is as fleeting as the shadows.

David's rising sense of frustration is revealed in stanza three. Despite the assertion of hope, David chides God for bringing him to such a sorry state. Finally, in desperation and faced with the prospect of imminent death, David begs God to let him have some few moments of happiness before he dies. The Psalms generally reflect the traditional theology of hope; this psalm, however, more than any other, reveals the uncommon theology of despair.

A New Song on My Lips (Psalm 40)

Here is a psalm of two distinctly different parts, thought by some observers to be two psalms. The first part (verses 1-10) is a joyous hymn of thanksgiving and the second (verses 11-17) is a cry for help and one verse of praise. If we agree that these are two parts of the same psalm, it might be interpreted as a song of profound gratitude for deliverance from deep distress which the psalmist recalls and relates in the second part.

In stanza one, the psalmist is singing a new song of happiness at having been rescued. This is followed by a beatitude of trust in the Lord. The singer has turned away from a life of worshiping false gods and making ritual sacrifices. True happiness is to do the will of God with delight (verse 8). The joy of God's presence is then shared with the congregation (verses 9-10).

In the second part of this poem the psalmist is recalling his distress and the plea that was made for deliverance. It was a cry for help that was made by a person whose sins were causing unbearable suffering and whose enemies were taunting him unmercifully. Despite the agonies of this distressing state of affairs, the psalmist is still able to praise God and to anticipate deliverance.

The Joy of Service (Psalm 41)

The key line in this psalm of happiness is in the first verse—happy is the person who cares for the poor. The first of three sections of the psalm (verses 1-3) is a beatitude on the happiness and the rewards of serving the poor. Such persons can expect to live in the glowing presence of God and under divine protection.

In the second section (verses 4-9) the psalmist, who is clearly not the happy person of section one, recites a prayer of confession and enters a plea for grace. There follows a description of all the distress the psalmist has sustained, the most unbearable parts of which are the betrayal by a once good friend and the rumors of impending death.

Section three provides a happy ending. A gracious God has upheld the psalmist, restrained the enemy, and enveloped this supremely happy person with the divine presence forever.

Verse 13 is not related to this psalm. It is a doxology in the literary form of a beatitude which brings Book I of the Psalms to a close.

§ § § § § § §

The Message of Psalms 32–41

Happiness is blessedness in the language of most of the psalms in this part. And the pursuit of a state of blessedness (bliss) on earth was an essential characteristic of early Israel's religious experience. It is inappropriate, however, to equate the state of blessedness with constant pleasure and freedom from the necessary constraints of community and national life. Happiness is shown to be a state in which the godly life of moral restraints is lived with joy.

§ Happy is the person who is free from the worry caused by guilt.

§ Happy is the nation whose security is in God. Happy is the community which can praise God.

§ Happy are the people who fear the Lord.

§ Happy is the person who can be proved to be innocent of false accusations.

§ Happy are those who are faithful to God and have complete freedom from worry.

§ Happy are the people who have maintained their faith as the price of suffering.

§ Happy is one who has experienced God's loving salvation and deliverance.

§ Happy is the person who knows the joy of helping others.

§ § § § § § §

Psalms 42–51

Introduction to These Psalms

These ten songs exhibit remarkable diversity in both style and mood. Part Five opens with three poignant poems of deepest despair. Then the mood is abruptly altered with a song of exquisite beauty about a royal wedding. Following this are three majestic hymns of praise which speak to God's mighty powers of creation, sovereignty over all the world, and an earthly dwelling-place on Mount Zion. The last three poems offer instruction in matters of wealth, sacrifice, repentance, and renewal.

Loneliness and Despair (Psalm 42)

In the opinion of biblical scholars, this psalm and Psalm 43 were originally one psalm. The poetry flows naturally from one to the other. It is written by one who is in deep despair. Loneliness is also evident from the plaintive language of the first stanza. It may be that the psalmist is far from the comfort and solace of God's presence in the Temple on Zion. Estrangement from God is the lesson of the metaphor of the thirsty animals. Tears likened to food suggest deep sorrow. They taunt about God's failure to help (verse 3) is not unexpected in psalms where temporary despair is part of the story.

The mood seems more relaxed in verse 4 as the psalmist recalls the former days of glory when the people experienced joy in worship and excitement during the great religious festivals. So, despite the depth of misery and loneliness, God can still be praised from the hills in the far north where the psalmist is evidently being held captive. An interesting mythological concept is introduced in verse 7; *cataracts* (NRSV) *water falls* (NIV) are the rainstorms which break over the mountains as the waters are released from heaven to demonstrate the power of God.

Although God seems to have forgotten (verse 9), and the psalmist suffers from the taunts of the enemy, God is still awaited longingly, lovingly, and faithfully.

Send Out Your Light (Psalm 43)

The central figure of the preceding psalm has moved through despair to hope. Now, in the opening verse of this part of the poem, the psalmist begs for vindication and for transport to God's joyous presence at the Temple. The drama is heightened momentarily when it seems as if God has again abandoned the faithful servant. The result is a thoughtful (and familiar) petition for light and truth to serve as guideposts leading to Zion. Note the confidence that joy will be supreme when there is opportunity once again to kneel at the sacred altar.

But is all this simply wishful thinking or useless daydreaming? Sunk deep in misery, the psalmist cries because of the turmoil in his heart. Yet, even from the depths of despair, hope can emerge as long as faith is strong. Praise be to God!

Why Sleepest Thou? (Psalm 44)

This anthem of six stanzas is generally regarded as a national hymn of sorrow. Israel is suffering and once again God seems to have forgotten. The psalmist is pleading the nation's cause. The opening stanza is a recollection of earlier days when God seemed to care. It includes a reminder that Israel's forefathers did not rout their enemies nor win the victories by themselves. God was responsible for driving the Canaanites out of the promised land. In stanza two, the psalmist expresses confidence that God will continue to sustain the people now in the same way that it was done for Jacob. In this and other psalms, the names *Jacob* and *Israel* are synonyms.

With the opening lines of stanza three (verse 9) the psalmist comes immediately to the subject of the psalm. God has abandoned the nation and the results are calamitous, as verses 9-16 reveal. The psalmist's recital of misfortune is beyond belief. The scattering and selling of people (verses 11-12) may be a reference to the Exile.

In stanzas four and five the psalmist protests the way God has treated Israel despite the fact that the people have been faithful. They might have deserved such dire punishment had they actually been disloyal, but that was not the case. Although God has forgotten, they have not. Their harmless little sins cannot possibly be the cause of it all. There must be some other reason. Is it possible that the price of loyalty and faith is suffering? Is it in the nature of things that God expects faith to grow from distress?

The final stanza is a petition challenging God to rouse from sleep and deliver the nation from its disaster.

A Royal Wedding (Psalm 45)

The king in this poem may be Ahab, whose marriage to Jezebel is the subject of 1 Kings 16:31. The reference to Tyre (verse 12 in this psalm) implies that Jezebel, a daughter of the Zidonians (Sidon) may have been the young king's bride. The evil nature of Ahab's kingship is not in any way foretold by the text of this psalm.

A self-styled, fluent singer opens the ceremony, singing directly to the king. The description of the royal bridegroom is reminiscent of the earlier portrayals of David, in whose lineage this king is following. Two kingly responsibilities are expected of this monarch: leadership in battle (the warrior) and defense of the right (the judge).

In verses 6-9, the psalmist turns to the qualities that make the bridegroom the most favored of men. The enduring throne is Israel's heritage from David's time and the royal scepter is the national symbol of justice. The king's loyalty to God and the covenant is proved by his love of good and hatred of evil. Signs of royal splendor are the costly oils and spices. In the setting of an ivory palace he is surrounded by lovely young women, the daughters of kings from the region around Israel.

In verse 9*b* the words of the wedding song are directed to the queen. The queen may actually be the princess who is about to become queen. Her dress is a robe of gold from Ophir, an Arabian land east of the Red Sea. Verses 10-12 advise the princess of the obligations to her lord and her adopted country. The dowry comes from Tyre, one of the rich trading cities on the Phoenician coast.

With the preliminaries cared for, the psalmist then provides a vivid picture of the wedding procession (verses 13*b*-15). The final stanza (verses 16-17) contains uncertainties about whom the psalmist is addressing and whether the words are the psalmist's alone or spoken in the name of God. However, the message seems clear enough. The male children of this king and queen will become celebrated princes.

A Hymn of Faith (Psalm 46)

This powerful poem was the inspiration for Martin Luther's great Christian hymn "A Mighty Fortress Is Our God." The psalm is a composition of three stanzas, beginning with a declaration of complete trust in God even if cataclysmic changes (earthquakes and floods) should occur in the earth. By citing potential disasters of such proportion, the psalmist may be imagining the end of the world, although that concept (eschatology) is rarely introduced into the Psalms.

The second stanza of this hymn reveals the psalmist's continued affirmation of trust. The river (verse 4) is doubtless the river of life which flows from Zion, God's earthly home. The nation of Israel, which is fortunate to have God dwelling in its midst, can feel very secure even though other nations are tottering and crumbling. A congregational response (verse 7) completes the stanza. It reveals a strong sense of national security. The line is a wonderful statement of trust.

In the last stanza the congregation is invited to think about the deeds God has done, with power and authority, to bring eternal peace. Then, with one of the great literary gems of history (verse 10), the psalmist sings God's words, *Be still, and know that I am God.* It is a stirring moment. The hymn closes with the congregational refrain, a repetition of verse 7.

King of Kings (Psalm 47)

The central theme of this poem is the universal sovereignty of God. A traditional understanding of this theme among the people of Jacob (Israel) is that all of history is ruled by their God. It is only a matter of time until nations everywhere understand this.

Verses 1-4 are a call to praise, reminding the people that God gave them their homeland. When the Most High is described as *awesome terrible,* it means that the mighty acts of history brought terror to the heathens and enemies.

Stanza two portrays the tradition of bearing the ark of the covenant to the Temple with joyous song and sounding of the shophar, a ram's horn trumpet. The processional was symbolic of God's entry into Zion.

The final stanza is a declaration of God's sovereignty over all the world as the princes of the nations, who are the *shields* of verse 9, gather before the throne.

Zion, the Holy Mountain (Psalm 48)

Here is a great hymn of praise, a tribute to God who dwells on Mount Zion. The city of Jerusalem is set in a shallow valley protected by hills rising on three sides. But the sense of protection here is not geographic. The best defense is the presence of God in Zion.

The first of four stanzas joyfully praise God's presence. The curious reference to the *far north* (NRSV) or *utmost heights* (NIV) is probably a fragment of mythology from the Canaanites whose god lived in the north.

A recitation of some of God's mighty acts in history comprises stanza two. Heathen kings panicked at the presence of God, trembling as if they were women in labor. Shattering of ships of Tarshish was probably a frequent disaster for the people of the coastal areas of the Mediterranean Sea. God's supreme act, for Israel, was the establishment of the house in Zion.

Verses 9-11 echo the praise of stanza one. The words are joyful strains of Israel's hope that God's name will be known everywhere. The final stanza provides a description of the physical attributes of the Temple on Mount Zion. But its principal message is that Israel must educate its people to keep this crucial tradition alive. Zion is actually God's presence and all generations must know this.

God and Mammon (Psalm 49)

This psalm of five stanzas is an anthem of wisdom on the religious theme that the love of money is the root of evil. We are reminded of a passage from the Sermon on the Mount (see Matthew 6:24). The words of this psalm are arranged by one who must have been a teacher. Recital of the poem is ritualistic drama set to music. Stanza one is the prologue to the proverbs which comprise the remainder of the psalm.

The first proverb (stanza two) takes the form of question and answer. Why should one fear the wicked? One need not fear the wicked, despite their prosperity. Riches cannot help secure God's blessings. Moreover, no amount of wealth can enable one to live forever.

The second proverb (verses 10-15) says that all must die someday and cannot take their riches to their graves with them. But the distinction drawn by the teacher here separates the wicked from the godly person. Those who have confidence in riches rather than in God will die the death of animals and spend their death in Sheol. But those whose faith is in God and not in their lust for wealth will abide in God's presence forever. This proverb alludes to eternal life (verse 15), but it does not reflect a New Testament concept of heaven. It refers to the feeling that God's presence will remain.

The idea that God can ransom the soul hints at the destiny of Jesus (Matthew 10:28). One happy note appears in the last stanza. Although death is certain and without doubt final, glory and perhaps praise for a good life and honor for a good reputation will live on as future generations remember righteous people.

The Nature of Sacrifice (Psalm 50)

This psalm deals with the essential question of what God requires of Israel in the way of sacrifices. The psalmist prefaces that inquiry with a vivid description of how God's divine nature is revealed. The revelations are known as *theophany*. A kindred word, *epiphany*, is a Christian festival celebrated on January 6. Epiphany celebrates the manifestation of the divinity of Jesus.

God shines from Zion with power symbolized by the sun. God does not exhibit power in silence, as the raging tempests and fires reveal. In Israel's ritual of covenant renewal, the faithful must gather before God in order to judged. In this way, the divine nature is revealed and the entire universe witnesses it.

In the second stanza, God is declared to be God. There is no need for animal sacrifices because all the animals belong to God anyway. An additional rebuke follows in the third stanza (verses 12-13), but then God tells the people that renewal of loyalty is expected and that the only sacrifice required is simple thanksgiving. All that God requires is loyalty and trust.

The remainder of the psalm discusses God's rebuke of the wicked. The psalmist speaks for God, who lists the sins of the wicked and lays the charge on them. In the final verse, they are given one last chance to repent.

Whiter Than Snow (Psalm 51)

This is one of the great penitential psalms of Christendom. It is useful in ritual as a prayer of cleansing and forgiveness. Apparently it is based on Nathan's rebuke of David following the episode with Uriah and Bathsheba (2 Samuel 12:1-14). David prays for mercy and petitions God to wash away his sins. He is very much aware of his sinful nature and, having repented, he voices his approval of God's judgment. The sin of his mother (verse 5) is not a condemnation of her; it is an acknowledgment of the doctrine of original sin.

As the prayer continues David recognizes the importance of truth in his heart and seeks God's wisdom in order to find the truth. Again he begs for God's cleansing power, hoping to become whiter than snow. Hyssop was evidently a plant grown regionally which had some uses in the rites of purification. It was also used medicinally. The prayer goes on to include a request that bones be healed. This is probably said figuratively. In all likelihood, David's mental image of himself was of a person badly broken in spirit by shame.

With verses 10-12, the psalm takes on a new mood of joy. It is as if David feels deeply the forgiving presence of God and a wonderful new sense of having been washed clean and restored to favor. In consequence of God's merciful act of deliverance, David promises to teach others the moral precepts which are now governing his new life (verses 13-14).

David concludes this prayer with three of the psalm's most beautiful lines. They could have been composed only by a very humble person who loved God intensely and who had been made completely whole by the depth of the purification experience.

The concluding lines (verses 18-19) about rebuilding Jerusalem were evidently added during the compiling of the Psalter long after the destruction of the Temple and the Babylonian captivity.

§ § § § § § §

The Message of Psalms 42–51

This group of psalms exhibits wide diversity in both style and approach. It does not seem to have a theme around which a single message might be written. There is, however, an interesting mixture of biblical history and ethical teachings. Admonitions, proverbs, prayers, and ritual sentences are included, as are some very lovely verses worth memorizing as gems of biblical literature.

§ Lonely and desolate people may find strength to endure their trials by waiting patiently for God.

§ Pray earnestly for light and truth as guideposts to living.

§ If it seems that God has forgotten when national disaster strikes, it may be that through the ordeals faith will be made stronger.

§ The wedding of a king is the occasion for remembrance of the king's obligation and the importance of perpetuating the house and lineage of David.

§ Trusting that God is a fortress sustains people even though the earth may undergo cataclysms.

§ Israel's traditions held that God is the governor of the entire universe. The seat of government is Zion.

§ Wealth cannot enable one to live forever. Those whose confidence is in wealth rather than God will surely die.

§ God does not require of Israel that animals be sacrificed. God requires only loyalty and thanksgiving.

§ People who trust God and repent of their sins may be wholly cleansed. Understanding God's moral precepts is essential to such purification.

§ § § § § § §

Psalms 52–61

Introduction to These Psalms

The theme of these psalms is the determination to trust God regardless of events. Even in the most difficult circumstances the writers provide some hint of God's ultimate goodness. The historic inclinations toward hope and trust are deeply embedded in the Hebrew consciousness, and revealed in rich variety in these psalms.

Coping with Treachery (Psalm 52)

The basis of the story is recorded in 1 Samuel 21:1-9. The psalmist begins by denouncing a wicked, deceitful person (verses 1-4). Evidently, the one being addressed has some wealth and a prominent social position. But this individual is known to be a vicious, boastful braggart and a treacherous liar who defies God's moral precepts.

With verses 5-7, the psalmist issues warnings to this wicked person about the certainty of divine judgment. God will bring the boastful, lying sinner to destruction. When that happens the righteous can rejoice, not vindictively but with appreciation for the reliability of God's judgments. The moral here is that it is folly to put one's trust in a refuge of riches rather than in the refuge of God.

In the final stanza (verses 8-9), the psalmist provides a personal testimony. It is an eloquent monologue emphasizing enduring trust in God. With a very pretty metaphor, the green olive tree grown inside homes and in the Temple precincts becomes a symbol of stability as well as God's life-giving presence.

A prayer of thanksgiving is offered for what God has done (verse 9), although it is not made clear what God has done. Very likely the psalmist may be thinking it to be effective judgment against treachery and deceit.

God Is! (Psalm 53)

This psalm is almost identical to Psalm 14. Here the writer uses *God* instead of LORD. The change appears to be editorial, introduced at some later date during the compilation of the Psalter. There are also some differences as one compares the text and the numbering of verses in the last stanzas of the two psalms.

In verse 5 of this psalm, the people are assured that God will completely destroy the ungodly ones who are not part of the community of faith. A petition for the delivery of Israel is offered (verse 6*a*). When God responds (verse 6*b*), Israel can again rejoice.

A Cry for Help (Psalm 54)

Here is a typical prayer of lament. David has written it, probably from memories of the terror he felt at having to hide from Saul. The event is recorded in 1 Samuel 23:19.

The prayer opens with an anguished cry for help. David calls on the *name* of God. *Name* signifies divine power. Verse 2 is the traditional Hebrew form of address to God. David's immediate concern is the godless, insolent (irreverent) enemy who is intent upon killing him.

The declaration of trust (verses 4-5) is forthright. David is certain that God will bring the enemy to destruction. The final stanza (verses 6-7) deals with the sacrificial thanksgiving which God requires. The concept of the freewill offering is a familiar one. It implies that the sacrifice is made willingly, stirred by the loving impulses of the heart. Evidently David understands that ritual sacrifices of burnt animals are no longer necessary.

Verse 7 is a glowing statement of confidence. From his experiences, David knows that God is unfailing. Doubtless he is remembering an earlier confrontation with the Philistines. The psalm concludes with the assertion that God's help has allowed him to see his enemies defeated. The statement should be interpreted as humble gratitude and not as vindictiveness.

God Sustains Us (Psalm 55)

This psalm is a personal lament, with a structure different from the more routine pattern. The moods within the seven stanzas change, often abruptly, among prayerful petitions, cries of anguish, calls for vengeance and retribution, and proverbs of wise counsel.

The psalm begins with the petition of a deeply troubled person. The psalmist is asking God to hear a pitiful recital of heartache and misery. The troubles are of such magnitude that the only recourse is to flee, to get away to a wilderness of peace and quiet.

Because of enemies a serious crisis has developed. The mental anguish is excruciating, and the days are filled with terror and the dread of death. Then from the depths of despair comes the inspiration for one of the more beautiful verses in the Bible—the metaphor of the wings of a dove! Verses 6-8 are a wistful hope that the wilderness environment would somehow alleviate the suffering.

In stanza three, the psalmist again offers a petition, this time for the salvation of the city. It is full of corruption; the marketplace is a center of fraud and deceit and the walls are infested with evil enemies. And worst of all, one of those enemies was once a trusted friend (verses 11-12). In consequence of total frustration over these terrible circumstances, the psalmist utters a plea for the death of the enemies. Then with a brisk change of mood, the psalmist recites a passionate prayer for deliverance from these enemies who do not revere the Lord. At this point, the picture of the deceitful friend is recalled and the mental anguish begins all over again. It is not difficult to imagine the depth of distress over that betrayal. The psalmist is portraying a person who simply cannot forget the grievances of the past. The metaphors of butter and oil provide an interesting touch.

With another swing of mood, a familiar verse of scripture is inserted. Perhaps it is a Temple priest who recites this captivating oracle (verse 22). It is followed by another declaration of trust. But somehow, this psalmist cannot resist the temptation to take another thrust at the cause of the anguish, the hated enemies.

I Trust in God (Psalm 56)

Here is another psalm in the format typical of the lament. The setting is apparently the same as that for Psalm 34, recorded in 1 Samuel 21:10-12. Four stanzas comprise the text. The first is the cry for help. The repetitive figures of speech suggest deep anxiety even though confidence in God is explicitly affirmed in verses 3-4.

Verses 5-6 depict the almost demonic behavior of enemies. It is difficult to imagine why their persecution is felt so intensely. Perhaps the king is speaking and exhibiting the effect of pressures of military campaigns.

Beginning with verse 6b, the psalmist seeks the defeat of these troublesome enemies. God knows of the problems making life so difficult. The picturesque metaphors of tears in bottles and a book of records illustrate the extent of God's knowledge and care.

A complete statement of trust is then introduced, including an echo of the refrain appearing in verse 4. The last stanza is a heartfelt prayer of thanksgiving. Once again, God has entered directly into human affairs to rescue a faithful servant from the grasp of death. Verse 13b comes from the heart of a truly grateful believer.

Shadow of Your Wings (Psalm 57)

The theme of this psalm is mercy. Using the lovely metaphor of sheltering wings, the psalmist makes a declaration of trust. The sheltering wings allude to the care of a brooding bird for her young. A petition is offered to God for help. In those sentences is a clear implication that a positive response is expected.

In verse 4, the ghastly imagery points toward some immediate danger, probably from demonic influences. As if to emphasize the extent of fear and to be assured that God is listening, the psalmist breaks into a song of praise (verse 5). It is also possible that verse 5 was introduced later as a congregational refrain. In any event, rescue is prompt and dramatic as enemies now become entwined in their own snares (verse 6).

Because the initial cry for mercy has been answered so readily, a hymn of praise is sung. It is laden with rich figures of speech. Musicians are summoned to greet the new day. Awakening the dawn may indicate a recollection of a mythological winged goddess who appeared with the rising of the sun to preside over the beginning of each new day. The joyous song of praise offered in verse 5 is repeated as the climax of this joyful psalm.

The God Who Judges (Psalm 58)

This is one of the Psalter's great dramatic monologues. Its language is vehement. The opening lines address a company of supernatural beings who are charged with corruption. The psalmist is, of course, speaking for God. Were these gods to look down they would see a debauched earth, the consequence of their misdoings.

Verses 3-5 picture the wicked of the earth as lying, venomous, despicable sinners. A strongly worded petition comprises the remainder of the psalm. Its word pictures are among the most vivid in all the Psalms.

Breaking teeth is a metaphor for quieting down the young lions, unbelievers professing no loyalty to God. Asking that they vanish like water is hoping that they will disappear just as if they had never been born. Similarly, the slime of the snail in verse 8 was at one time thought to be evidence of its body's gradual dissolution. Verse 8b suggests a miscarriage or stillbirth.

Another metaphor (verse 9) compares the ungodly to the righteous using trees. The wood of the thorn tree, more properly a weedy shrub, was used as a cooking fuel. It ignited easily and was consumed quickly with a hot flame. The ungodly are like that. They are consumed quickly and then are gone forever. But the righteous are like the green tree, difficult to ignite and slow to burn.

The vehemence of the language is still evident in the final stanza. Righteous people do not really wish to exact vengeance in a bloodbath. The vengeance the psalmist is really thinking about is more likely to be God's exercise of justice, as verse 11 clearly implies.

God Is My Fortress (Psalm 59)

The setting of this story may be David's home. Saul's henchmen are approaching with orders to kill him. That episode is recorded in 1 Samuel 19:11-18. It is clearly an appeal for deliverance, as indicated in the opening prayer. This is followed by a protest of innocence and a request of God to wake up and punish the evil offenders. The distress is reiterated as the vigor and intensity of the language increase. Verse 6 likens the evil ones to fearful wild animals of the night. The question about who can hear in verse 7 is the ridicule of a godly person by scornful unbelievers. Yet the psalmist is convinced that God will hear and that action will be taken to subdue the enemy.

In verses 11-12 the psalmist proposes that the lives of the enemy be spared. The reason is that their downfall and public humiliation will serve as an example to the people. Yet another reason is to demonstrate that God is sovereign in the universe (verse 13). Verses 14-15 repeat the substance of verses 6-7 and are extraneous here.

An affirmation of trust brings the psalm to its climax in the final stanza. The mention of the morning may relate this poem to an element of worship. If so, it is a jubilant finale to the troubled events of the night before.

A National Crisis (Psalm 60)

Israel has suffered a catastrophic military defeat. The nation and its people are humiliated and broken in spirit. The opening lines of the psalm are a melancholy lament, a recital of the dreadful events that have transpired. Somehow the nation has angered God enough that the people are in total disarray and behaving as if they were in a drunken stupor.

Suddenly an ensign is raised (verse 4). It gives the people an indication that they may be spared further military reverses. Additional evidence for optimism is provided by the recall of an ancient oracle. Its recitation reminds the nation that God once gave them the land as well as dominion over their neighbors. The glossary in this commentary identifies the approximate locale of the places recorded in verses 6-8. The neighboring nations of Moab and Edom were not under Israel's dominion; hence they were given the more menial portions of this metaphorical kingly array, the washbasin and the shoe box.

Following the oracle, the psalmist makes another appeal for help. The nation's armies are reorganizing for an assault on the Edomites. Israel has learned an important lesson (verses 10-11). No military activities will again be attempted unless God is with them.

God Will Listen (Psalm 61)

Israel's king (perhaps it is David) is in distress. It may be physical illness if the *end(s) of the earth* (verse 2) is understood to be the entrance to Sheol (death). On the other hand, the king's misery may be the mental pressures of administering a government. The supplication is to be taken to a secure place, and only God can do this. The most appealing haven is God's tent or tabernacle, meaning the Temple, where there are cleansing and healing rituals. The beautiful metaphor *shelter of your wings* (verse 4) suggests the figure of the protective mother bird caring for her young. It is symbolic of the security and perfect trust one may feel in the presence of God in the *tent*.

Verse 5 underscores an interesting characteristic of perfect trust. Completely confident of affirmative response, the psalmist assumes that God has already answered almost before the prayers were uttered.

The final stanza (verses 6-8) is a prayer for the king. In the ritual of Temple worship, the choir would sing this prayer accompanied by the lyre. The prayer is an echo of God's promise to David (Psalm 2) that his lineage will be perpetuated forever. May God be praised.

§ § § § § § §

The Message of Psalms 52–61

Throughout these psalms, trust in God is the dominant theme. That trust is the pillar of Israel's religious beliefs and experiences and it is fundamental to a king's performance of royal obligations in peace or war. These poems demonstrate that trust in God is also essential to personal security and peace of mind.

§ God can be trusted to judge the wicked regardless of their prestige, power, and wealth.

§ Israel discovered that God did fulfill promises to destroy evil.

§ God can be trusted to provide unfailing support for the king.

§ How difficult it is to forget insults and injuries. Not to forget implies that one cannot quite trust God.

§ Psalms of lament almost invariably include a statement of trust and confidence in God.

§ God can be trusted to judge with equity.

§ God is always a trustworthy refuge.

§ § § § § § §

Psalms 62–72

Introduction to These Psalms

The psalms in this part are stories of joys and sorrows. But they all imply or reveal trust in God and gratitude for God's faithfulness. Psalms of gratitude often contain remembrance of pain, suffering, or alienation from God. But they also tell of one's appreciation for deliverance, for reconciliation, for fulfillment of the obligations of the covenant, and for steadfast love. In some of these psalms, feelings of gratitude are expressed as pure joy and delight. Israel used the psalms of gratitude during its great festivals celebrating the harvests, the coming of the new year, and covenant renewal.

Power Belongs to God (Psalm 62)

The psalm opens with verses of confidence in God. They are a prelude to a confrontation with enemies who are addressed directly (verse 3) with a question of how long a king must put up with their harassment. David then portrays their lying, deceitful attitudes and their efforts to dethrone him (verse 4).

In verses 5-6, the opening declaration of confidence is repeated. Here it is a prelude to a fuller exposition of the depth of David's trust in God (verse 7) and his wise counsel to the people, advising them also to trust and confide in God (verse 8).

David then delivers an exhortation (verses 9-10) on the folly of trusting in human nature and in material wealth.

Setting one's heart on increasing riches appears to be little better than extortion and robbery. The final stanza is written in the form of a proverb to the effect that mighty, divine acts in history, tales of which David has heard repeated, reveal that power does indeed belong to God.

Thirsting for God (Psalm 63)

Composition of this psalm may have occurred during David's passage into the wilderness as he fled from Absalom (2 Samuel 15:23). A wilderness setting is suggested by the language of stanza one as David longs for God and offers a declaration of praise. The second stanza (verses 5-8) is a meditation on the rich blessings of security under God's watchful care. It is as if David has been filled with the best foods available. His safety is assured and, using the familiar word pictures of God's wings and hands, he makes his gratitude clearly evident.

The flight from Absalom has apparently kept David mindful of his enemies, but his confidence in God's power to destroy them is complete (verses 9-10). Verse 11 is David's promise that his people will be faithful to God.

The Righteous Rejoice (Psalm 64)

The poetry is divided into three distinct parts, the first being six verses of bitter complaint about enemies. Their actions are told in some detail and include their own self-congratulatory words about their ability to plot and scheme and to lay traps and snares. Despite these apparent successes, their victim, the psalmist, knows that God is aware of their deviousness. Not only will their secret thoughts be known, but God will also bring them to ruin (verse 8). And once this is done the people will know what has happened to the enemy. It will be understood by all that God has rendered judgment according to previous promises. The song closes with a jubilant summons to the faithful to rejoice. It is a fitting expression of gratitude for God's loving care.

Thanksgiving Day (Psalm 65)

Here is a beautiful song of thanksgiving. The first stanza is a hymn of praise, expressing loyalty to God and thanks for listening to prayer and for remitting sins. A grateful people are also acknowledging their satisfaction with the wonderful experiences of living in the presence of God and of worshiping in the Temple.

Stanza two is a prayer that recognizes God's saving act when the turbulence of the physical world was brought under control and made to function with predictable regularity. The most conspicuous example is the rising of the sun and the setting of the same (verse 8). The crucial events of Genesis 1, the creation of mountains, seas, and humanity are the consequences of God's strength (verses 6-7). The people who dwell apart from God's presence and who do not have Israel's knowledge of these events are naturally frightened by them (verse 8).

In the final stanza, the people offer their gratitude to God for the richness of the earth. Evidently the psalm was written at the time of the autumn rains, as the showers indicate (verse 10). The harvest is bountiful; the wagons bearing the produce of the fields are heavily laden. Even the areas of land that are not under cultivation are enriched with ripeness. All this lush vegetation has provided more than enough food for the flocks. Little wonder that the people shout and sing for joy!

Truly God Has Listened (Psalm 66)

God has listened to the cries of Israel throughout a long, dramatic, and sometimes catastrophic history. This psalm is written in remembrance of part of that history. As the psalmist begins, the first stanza bids the congregation to sing joyfully and praise God for *awesome deeds* that cause fear in the hearts of the enemy. In the second stanza (verses 5-7) the psalmist remembers God's use of fearful power when the waters were parted during the Exodus (Exodus 14–15).

The third stanza is a reminder to the people that throughout their history they have been punished by their oppressors, subjected to great misfortunes, and tested and purified like silver in the refiner's fire. Despite all of the tribulations, they are still God's people, safe in a *place of abundance* (NIV) or *spacious place* (NRSV). The place may be the land of Canaan where Israel's wilderness journey ended. Perhaps, in a wider context, it may mean liberty and freedom at any time in the nation's history.

Stanza 4 (verses 13-15) is the psalmist's promise to prepare and present an elaborate thanksgiving offering in the tradition of animal sacrifice. The lavish number of animals to be offered is poetic exaggeration. The more important aspect of the psalmist's song of gratitude is the testimonial (verses 16-19). The power of God that brought Israel through days of deepest distress with mighty acts of salvation is the same power that sustains individual persons (verse 16) and assures us that prayer is answered. Verse 20 is one of the more beautiful beatitudes in all of the Psalms.

God's Face Shines (Psalm 67)

Verse 1 of this psalm will be instantly recognized as the words of a lovely choral amen in frequent use at the close of Christian services of worship. The entire poem is a prayer of great gratitude, structured in versicles rather than complete stanzas. Two themes are found in the poetry. They are the reasons for the congregation's gratitude. One deals with God's presence. A radiant, shining countenance looks down on the world's peoples as they are judged with equity. The other has to do with God's wonderful generosity to people through rich harvests.

This psalm was used in ritual celebration. It was sung antiphonally by the choir (verses 1-2, 4, and 6-7) and the congregation (verses 3 and 5). Perhaps a final refrain for the congregation, possibly a verse 8, was lost during the process of accumulating the Psalter centuries ago.

Twelve Little Poems (Psalm 68)

This psalm does not seem to be a psalm at all. It is an assortment of unrelated verses. Scholars are not in agreement about the origin of these lines or why they were included in the Psalter. But the presence of the psalm here justifies an attempt to interpret it. The organization into twelve fragments is rather arbitrary and serves only the purpose of developing this commentary. Other writers would create different arrangements.

The first little poem (verses 1-3) is a call to praise and a word of fervent hope that enemies will receive God's judgment. *Smoke* is the figurative expression of the wish that the enemies will disappear quickly so that the righteous may bask in the brilliance of God's grace and goodness.

The second poem (verses 4-5) is another familiar call to praise. Its appearance at this point in the text suggests that it may have been part of a catalog of special verses rather than a psalm. The third poem (verses 6-7) describes two of God's important interests: care for the widows and orphans and provision of shelter for the desolate and oppressed. The *prisoners* may be the people of the Exodus.

The fourth little poem (verses 8-10) is an oracle recalling God's mighty acts following the Exodus from Egypt. The ultimate act was the restoration of Israel in the land of Canaan. Poem five (verses 11-13) pictures a great military victory. The writer is remembering Deborah's song (Judges 5:1-12). The figure of the dove symbolizes consistent longing for peace.

The sixth poem (verses 14-16) is a spirited defense of the choice of Zion as God's earthly home. The other mountains are belittled for not being selected. In poem seven (verses 17-18) God makes a triumphant entry into Jerusalem to establish a home on Mount Zion. The eighth poem (verses 19-20) is a beatitude praising God's acts of saving grace. The ninth little poem (verses 21-23) is a vehement denunciation of enemies whom God will surely destroy. The *hairy crown* refers to long hair, uncut for ritual reasons. The Lord will return the enemies from all over the earth (from Bashan to the seas) in order that they can be judged. The imagery of blood and dogs' tongues is obviously hyperbole. It refers to the death of the enemy. The tenth little poem (verses 24-27) describes a procession of victory, perhaps on the occasion of a festival. The leader was of the tribe of Benjamin, probably traditionally accorded that honor because Israel's first king, Saul, was a Benjaminite. Poem eleven (verses 28-31) is a prayer for final victory when all the earth's peoples will be brought together under the universal sovereignty of God. The beasts are symbols of wars which will cease. The end of tribute money payments points to the final eradication of corruption in the marketplaces. Bronze from Egypt is symbolic of the submission of all nations to the will of Israel's God.

The twelfth poem (verse 32-35) is a stirring call to praise. It includes fragments of mythology. God rides the heavens and speaks with a voice of thunder. *Awesome is God* (NRSV) or *you are awesome, O God* (NIV) indicates that God's power inspires reverence among the nations.

God Will Save Zion (Psalm 69)

The lengthy psalm is in the form of a lament. It begins with an agonizing cry of despair (verses 1-3). The muddy setting is identified with Sheol, implying that death is imminent. Stanza two portrays the enemy with characteristic exaggeration. God must surely know that the vicious accusations are false.

A special concern of the psalmist is that, if God chooses to ignore the cry for help, the people will lose faith (verses 6-9). A reminder is then addressed to God to the effect that all these indignities are sustained by the psalmist because of loyalty to God (for God's sake). Further suffering, also for God's sake, has now become the subject of idle gossip around the city (verses 10-12). In verses 13-15 a gentler approach is taken as the psalmist turns to prayer for rescue from certain death in the mire of Sheol (verses 13-15). In the petition which follows the presence of God is fervently sought. Guilt is readily admitted. It is followed by an account of extraordinary tribulation for which no solace is to be found anywhere in the city (verses 16-18). The lines in verses 19-21 are prophetic of Christ's suffering. The psalmist, now overcome by the torment, turns again to seek God's judgment on the hated adversaries. Verses 22-28 are a set of pungent, vitriolic sentences uttered, obviously, by a tortured soul in frustration and despair.

The mood changes abruptly in the next stanza. Assured that God will deal appropriately with the enemy and elevate his spirit (verse 29), the psalmist concludes the poem with the usual hymn of praise. It consists of two stanzas, the first affirming that God requires a sacrifice of thanksgiving, not animals. The second seeks the people's praise to God who will restore Judah and rebuild the cities, making them habitable for those who love God's name.

O Lord, Do Not Tarry (Psalm 70)

This psalm is identical to verses 13-17 of Psalm 40. It is a cry for help sounded by a person whose enemies' taunts are unmerciful. Despite the agonies of this distressing predicament, the psalmist is still able to praise God and to anticipate deliverance. However, there is a hope that God will not wait too long.

Do Not Forsake Me (Psalm 71)

This gentle complaint by an elderly person is different from the typical lament. The first stanza is one of confidence and gratitude that God is still a strong fortress. Yet some special protection seems to be required from enemies whose threats are included among the words of praise (stanzas 2-3). The combination of fear, confidence, and hope continues in the fourth stanza (verses 12-16) which the psalmist concludes with words of praise. The tone of the poetry becomes steadily more poignant through the fifth and sixth stanzas. In a sense, the psalm seems less a lament here and more like a song of acceptance of what life is offering. At the same time, this person, displaying quiet, peaceful composure, is continuing to praise God in tranquil expectation that God will never forsake one so demonstrably loyal. It is a beautiful expression of attitudes that only a human being full of years can hope to possess.

A Moral Testament (Psalm 72)

The authorship of this psalm is in dispute among biblical scholars. There are tempting reasons to believe that the poem may have actually been written by David in anticipation of Solomon's succession to the throne. One could readily understand that, at the end of a successful reign, David would want to share the accumulated wisdom and art of government. Another interpretation has associated the poem with the sovereignty of God, assuming that the earthly king would perform kingly duties with God as the model. In any case, the psalm is a remarkable statement of public policy for the people of Jacob.

Six irregular stanzas comprise the psalm, the first of which comes directly to one of God's most important precepts. The inclusion of the poor, the needy, and the oppressed among those for whom justice is intended is evidence of a remarkably modern conception of democratic principles in action.

The sentiment in stanza two is enthralling. It seems appropriate to expect a leader to create an atmosphere that bears similarities to God's lovely, natural world. In the third stanza, the significant Hebrew concept of the universal sovereignty of God is advanced. Tarshish, a city situated probably on the coast of what is now Spain, represented the western extremity of the known world as the River (Euphrates) marked its boundary in the east. Stanza four is added for emphasis; it simply reiterates the demanding moral postulates which shaped the rich quality of Israel's community life.

In verses 15-17 our attention is directed to the personal fortunes of the king and the prosperity of his people. The prayer is brought to a close by a pair of matchless beatitudes exalting the God of Israel.

Verse 20 is not a part of this psalm. It is a kind of doxology marking the end of Book II of the Psalms.

§ § § § § § §

The Message of Psalms 62–72

The love of God in the hearts of the early Israelite peoples is seldom reflected any more joyously than in this group of psalms, where gratitude and thanksgiving are the dominant themes. The people accepted what life offered them because they understood clearly that their existence was in accord with God's intentions. These poems reveal a deep sense of gratitude that grew among them as they came to understand more fully what the special relationship with God meant to them.

§ God's nature is more reliable than human nature.

§ Thank God for the special care that is provided for the reigning monarch.

§ Thank God for shielding the people from enemies who lurk all around.

§ Thank God for a radiant presence in the Temple.

§ Thank God for being a good listener.

§ Thank God for administering divine justice.

§ Thank God for a homeland for the chosen people.

§ Thank God for instituting an earthly home on Mount Zion and for living there among the people of Israel.

§ § § § § § §

Psalms 73–80

Introduction to These Psalms

The covenant between God and Israel is cited a number of times in the Psalms. To emphasize its importance in Israel's history we shall use the covenant as the central theme of this group of psalms. It was crucial to the life and times of the people who were the actors in these poetic dramas. A comprehensive view of the covenant follows the Ten Commandments (Exodus 20:22–23:33). All the psalms in this part are songs of Asaph. They are probably from a collection used by Temple singers. Asaph is identified as one of David's chief musicians.

Is Life Unfair? (Psalm 73)

The theme of this psalm is set forth in verse 3—envy of prosperous people. The envy the psalmist is feeling is a very human response when life is unfair. What makes life even more unfair in this psalm is the extraordinarily wicked lifestyle of the prosperous. Just how wicked these prosperous people are is revealed in the second stanza (verses 4-9).

For this psalmist the most bitter irony of all is the praise and honor being given by the people (verse 10) to these wicked, prosperous persons. These are the ones who are belittling the very idea that any of this should be of concern to God (verse 12). At this point the psalmist is in despair. Keeping the covenant and maintaining loyalty to God now appear, momentarily at least, to have been in vain (verses 13-14).

The lapse into despair ends quickly. In the fourth stanza the psalmist tells of being revived by entering the sanctuary and receiving understanding of why life seems to be unfair. The fate of the wicked is also divinely revealed (verses 18-20).

The opening lines of the fifth stanza are the psalmist's confession of a temporary lapse in understanding and faith (verses 21-22). This is followed by a firm declaration of restored confidence and renewed faith in God (verses 23-26). The final verses include two independent thoughts: reassurance that the ungodly will be destroyed and elimination of the psalmist's doubt. In a way, these verses make it clear that the covenant is intact.

Has God Forgotten Us? (Psalm 74)

The entire psalm is a lengthy appeal to God in behalf of the community. It laments the total destruction of the Temple and God's abandonment of the people. Enemies, presumably Babylonians, have desecrated and defiled God's dwelling place on Zion as well as sanctuaries all over the country.

The psalmist knows that there is no one capable of leading the people out of these dreadful circumstances (verses 9-11). The only possibility is that God can somehow be persuaded to do something. God's failure to assist the people is symbolized by the right hand tucked inside a garment; it cannot, in that position, act in their behalf.

In stanza four (verses 12-17) the psalmist recalls some ancient mythological dragons and other fierce creatures. Israel believed that God, in the act of Creation, destroyed these strange animals who were represented as the forces of chaos. Now this God of power has forgotten the people and the covenant which was established between them.

The final verses are a prayer for God's attention. It is urgent that God restore the covenant and lift up the oppressed. In so doing the criminals must be struck down. Verse 22 is in the form of a battle cry imploring God's action. It is God, as much as the people, who is being taunted and mocked by these destructive unbelievers. The clear implication throughout this psalm is that another of God's mighty acts is long overdue.

God Judges with Equity (Psalm 75)

This is the joyful song of a faithful person who understands God's gifts to Israel and who accepts the covenant. Grateful thanks are the subject of verse 1. To call on the name of God is to ask to live in God's radiant presence.

In response to that call, God's words are then heard in verses 2-3. The appointed time does not seem to indicate the last days of New Testament eschatology. More likely it is an instant of time when God will once again enter into the affairs of Israel. A tottering earth may signify political upheaval, but God covenants to keep the foundations *(pillars)* of both the physical world and the moral law from collapsing.

The psalmist resumes by reciting an oracle. Lifting up the horn compares the unbelievers to wild, horned cattle who toss their heads around and snort defiance. An *outstretched* (NIV) or *insolent neck* (NRSV) is stiff-necked pride. Verse 6 provides testimony that it is useless to expect justice to come from any part of the physical world. God judges not capriciously but with equity, putting down the wicked and lifting up the righteous. Up and down hint at balancing with the scales of justice.

The oracle continues with a line describing the cup of wrath, a form of punishment in the ancient Near East. The harshest punishment was to be forced to drink the poison to the last drop *(dregs)*.

In verses 9-10 the psalmist echoes the praise and thanksgiving of verse 1 and then addresses a final word of condemnation and warning to the wicked.

An Angry God (Psalm 76)

The anger of which God is capable is here identified with terror. When God established a home in Zion in the city of Jerusalem (*Salem* here may be poetic abbreviation), the weapons of war were destroyed (verse 3).

The psalmist elaborates on the power of God using word pictures to portray the capacity to disarm the military (verses 4-6). God has done these deeds evidently in some anger and doubtless with a lack of patience with war. That God can be angry is further intimated in verses 7-9. There we find a short treatise on judgment, the theme of which is God's wrath on the oppressors of the poor and needy. It should be noted that, while God makes a home in Zion, the acts of judgment are made from the vantage point of heaven (verse 8).

The final verses (10-12) are a curious mixture of praise, counsel, and warning. They are puzzling inclusions, variously interpreted. To be praised by wrath (verse 10) may mean that God can accept wrath from people, regarding it as praise, because angry people facing God have not all turned away as would the unbelievers. Even the defiant could accept God's justice with praise however grudgingly. The reference to *vow* (verse 11) is a word of counsel to practice the appropriate rituals, to bring gifts, and to live up to the agreements of the covenant. Verse 12 seems to suggest that all persons, regardless of political station, will suffer from God's anger. Even kings and princes are under obligation to the covenant.

Is God's Love Steadfast? (Psalm 77)

The poetry is in two distinct parts, the first being a meditation on the apparent absence of God's love in the psalmist's life. The second is a brief account of the deeds of the Lord in Israel's history. Some observers classify this psalm as a lament. But unlike laments which often feature victims with an overpowering fear of enemies and serious physical and mental disabilities, this psalm is concerned with spiritual alienation from God. We do not know with what the psalmist is afflicted as he cries for help (verses 1-2).

Instead of the more familiar denunciation of enemies, the psalmist reveals some inner concerns about broken relationships with God (verses 3-6). Obviously an inquiry is underway for some indication of what has gone wrong and what has caused this painful estrangement. The climax of part one is reached in verses 7-9 as six searching questions are asked. The fourth one (verse 8b) implies that the covenant may be forsaken forever. Verse 10 seems to convey the fact that all six questions, alas, have no other answer than Yes. God has indeed changed!

Now in deep sorrow, the psalmist struggles to achieve consolation by sweet recollections of some of the deeds God has done throughout Israel's history. The creation of the world out of the waters of chaos is remembered (verses 16-18). Equally important to the psalmist is the passage across the Red Sea (verse 19). The final recollection (verse 20) is the leadership of Moses and Aaron, implying perhaps the ordering of the Ten Commandments and the Book of the Covenant (Exodus 20-23).

God in History (Psalm 78)

This psalm provides a digest of some early events in Israel's long and turbulent history. The narrative is preceded by a prologue (verses 1-4) uttered by a teacher of history. The announced intention of speaking in *parables* and *dark sayings* (NRSV) or *hidden things* (NIV) (riddles) was to make that history known to the then-present generation of listeners. Verses 3-4 identify the source of historical information as the oral tradition.

The story begins with God's institution of the covenant and the commandments (verse 5). Instructions were provided (verses 6-7) so that all generations might be kept informed and would not forget to revere the law.

The people were also counseled not to be rebellious and unfaithful as the preceding generation was.

The story moves on, describing an incident with the Ephraimites not recorded elsewhere in the Bible. Perhaps the teacher is using it to show what happens when the covenant is ignored. In verses 12-16 the miracle of the Exodus is related. The wilderness experiences are examined in some detail in verses 17-31. Historical incidents to which they refer are found in passages throughout Exodus, Numbers, and Deuteronomy. The years in the wilderness were fraught with almost constant bickering and even rebellion. God's patience was tested not simply because of their discontent; they had witnessed miracles, manna from heaven, and water from rocks on Mount Horeb, for example. It was their insistence on more miracles and good works that tried God so severely and caused the uncommon loss of patience. The result was the slaying of the strongest men of Israel (verse 31).

What follows in verses 32-39 is an account of human behavior which is far from unusual. Punished by having lost their best men (verse 31), the wandering Israelites pretended to repent, praising God as their refuge. But all the while they continued their sinful, lying ways, and defied the provisions of the covenant. Having regained patience, God forgave their sins and extended compassion, remembering that they were only human (verse 39).

At verse 40 the wilderness history is resumed with descriptions of the period of slavery in Egypt prior to the exodus. Emphasis is on the plagues recorded in Exodus 7–12. These plagues are crucial to the history of Israel as evidence of God's saving acts. By the hands of Moses and Aaron, God made the rivers run with blood (Exodus 7:14-20), made frogs, flies, and locusts swarm over the land (Exodus 8:6; 8:24; and 10:14), and caused hail to destroy vegetation all over Egypt (Exodus 9:25). The *sycamores* (NRSV) of verse 47 are figs, as the NIV makes clear. Smiting the firstborn Egyptians (verse 51), the descendants of Ham, the third son of Noah, is God's final act before the departure from Egypt. The incident is recorded in Exodus 12:29-13:29, and follows the institution of the feast of the Passover.

In verses 52-55 there is a brief digest of the history of the entire period, from flight from Egypt to the crossing of the Jordan under Joshua (Joshua 3:17) and to the settlement of the tribes of Israel in Canaan.

The remainder of the psalm is not so much a history of specific episodes as it is a tale of continued rebellion by Israel, of more treachery and deceit, provoking God to anger as it did in the wilderness. The consequence is rejection of Israel (verses 61-62). But all is not lost. God awakes and saves Israel by routing its enemies. An account of the establishment of the monarchy under David is given in the final stanza.

The primary objective of this psalm is not necessarily Israel's history. It is the recounting of numerous instances of God's direct involvement in that history. Evidences of God's action make that history rich indeed.

Jerusalem Is in Ruins (Psalm 79)

The incidents in verse 1 of this psalm appear to be the result of a national military defeat at the hands of Babylonians. Verses 2-3 reveal the terrible consequences of war on a tragic, inhuman scale. Israel is now in total disarray.

In stanza two, the psalmist poses a question directly to God. Enemy nations have perpetrated this dreadful catastrophe. Why God has permitted this to happen to Israel is not clear.

The remainder of the psalm constitutes an appeal, the principal features of which are retribution and vengeance upon the enemies. The special tribulation Israel bears in this circumstance is the certainty that God's energies have not been directed toward the people who are faithful.

There is an acknowledgment that Israel may be at fault. Sins of the forefathers and the present generation are confessed (verses 8-9). But the critical question arises in verse 10. Should the horrible crimes recounted in stanza one go unpunished? If they do, what is the world to think of Israel's God (verse 10)? If only God will act in Israel's behalf to free the prisoners and punish the oppressors, then the nation will express its generous praise and thanksgiving.

Restore Us, O God (Psalm 80)

This psalm is another in a series in which God seems unwilling or unable to act in Israel's behalf. The nation, believing most sincerely that it has kept its promises of the covenant with God, is deeply disturbed. The psalmist here reflects the anxiety. Clearly, a disaster has occurred.

An appeal for restoration is voiced (verses 1-3). Included is praise to God using the metaphor of the shepherd enthroned as king. The cherubim flanked God's earthly throne, the ark of the covenant. The tribes of verse 2 were the direct descendants of Jacob and Rachel.

The question in verse 4 is not uncommon in these psalms. God has been angered and the people are weeping bitter tears, scorned by neighboring enemies. The plea for assistance is supplemented by reminders to God that at one time this great nation was favored.

The *vine* brought out of Egypt (verse 8) is Israel. It grew beautifully and prosperously in Canaan, with roots throughout the ancient Near East (verse 11). But now God has failed to protect Israel and enemies have successfully invaded the land (verse 13).

Here the appeal is renewed with additional descriptions of the ravaged land. Israel is desperate (verses 14-17). The plea to strengthen the *son of man* (NIV) or *the one* (NRSV) is made in behalf of the king.

This reference to the son is probably not prophetic, although Jesus may have been aware of this psalm when he described himself as the vine (John 15:1).

Israel vows never again to turn away from God (verse 18) once the king is restored and strengthened in the heritage of the monarchy (verse 17). The psalmist is evidently recalling the anointing of a king (Psalm 2). The last verse is a prayer refrain identical to verses 3-7 and perhaps 14, at least in intent.

§ § § § § § §

The Message of Psalms 73–80

Commentary on this group of psalms has focused on the covenant and the historic manifestations of God's faithfulness to it. There were occasions in Israel's history when serious doubts about God's faithfulness arose, particularly in times of national disaster. These psalms offer a rich source of inspiration as the prayers and pleas of the nation of Israel are answered, often in dramatic and exciting ways, by God's intervention into its history.

§ Though life seems unfair, God works to restore equity.

§ There are times in human events when God seems to have forgotten the people.

§ God's anger may be justified under certain circumstances.

§ God has entered directly into Israel's history on many occasions. The actions were sometimes destructive but seemed always to cleanse.

§ God rejected Israel a number of times when she violated the law and the covenant.

§ God was often blamed for the great national disasters that befell the nation of Israel.

§ § § § § § §

PART
NINE Psalms 81–89

Introduction to These Psalms

The psalms in this group are almost all songs of deep
sorrow that arise typically because of alienation from
God, the power of sin, and the actions of the ungodly.
Despite the mood of despondency which characterizes
these psalms, each has an important element of hope
which emerges again and again. It is a remarkable
cultural trait of the people of Israel. Hope is invariably
expressed as an expectation for a better life, not in
heaven but here on earth. It is a means of dealing with
sorrow. Psalms 84 and 87 are exceptions to the general
theme of sorrow.

Israel Would Not Listen (Psalm 81)

This psalm has three segments which do not seem to
be directly related. In the first stanza a psalmist bids the
people to rejoice and praise God with music. Evidently a
festival is in progress and the call to rejoice is timely.
This festival celebrates the fond remembrance of the
covenant's origins and may possibly be the occasion for
its annual renewal.

In verses 6-10 God speaks and recalls the relief from
slavery (carrying bricks) and delivery from Egypt. There
follows a reminder that the thunder over Sinai is God's
voice. The incident at Meribah is the miracle of water
gushing from the rock of Mount Horeb. God then

reinforces the commandment regarding other gods (verses 8-9) and promises to keep the people well fed.

In the third segment of this psalm God is still speaking and laments the fact that Israel has refused to listen. We do not know to what God is referring. It is probable that enemies are at work but they are not identified. Even so, God promises to subdue them and end Israel's sorrow. This would be celebrated by dining on the finest foods God could supply.

The Heavenly Council (Psalm 82)

A meeting of the heavenly council is called to order. God enters and immediately chastises the angels. Their actions in judging the people of earth are not in accord with God's moral laws, and the consequence is sorrow among the needy and the afflicted (verses 3-4).

The *they* of verse 5 appears to be the members of the heavenly council, who are apparently badly prepared for their tasks. The administration of justice all over the earth is corrupt enough to shake the earth.

The punishment these lesser gods (angels, perhaps) are to receive is to suffer death in the same way that earthly residents do. Concepts about the heavenly council, the forum from which God's judgments emerge, included the notion that its members were sons of God who were assured a kind of everlasting existence. It is different from the New Testament concept of heaven, which is not expressed in the poetry of the psalms.

Middle East Conflict (Psalm 83)

Some interesting historic insight into current political strife in the Middle East is found in this psalm. It opens with a plea to God to break silence. God's enemies are conspiring against Israel. Neighboring nations have forged an alliance that encircles the beleaguered cities of Judah. Who are the enemies? They are peoples who, throughout the history of Israel, have consistently sought to overrun the land. The locale of each member of the alliance is noted in the glossary of this commentary. The Ishmaelites are not identified with a specific locality. The word seems to be an umbrella term identifying people of a region much larger than the nations which have Israel under siege.

In verses 9-11 the psalmist prays to God for the kind of help that was given in earlier, successful struggles against invaders. The psalmist is recalling events recorded in Judges 4-8. Princes and kings named in verse 11 were slain at the hand of Gideon (Judges 7:25; 8:21).

The last stanza (verses 13-18) is an exhortation begging God to declare a judgment on the nations to bring all the powers of nature to bear on them so that they will perish from the face of the earth. If all of this can be done, all the nations will know that Israel's God is the universal sovereign.

Longing for Your Home (Psalm 84)

Nostalgia rather than sorrow or sadness is the mood in the first stanza. The psalmist is presumably a pilgrim longing for a reunion with God's living presence at the Temple. Just the thought of being there causes great elation and excitement.

Great tenderness is evident as the psalmist recalls God's care for the birds that nest near the Temple's altars. With some emotion a beatitude is sung for all the creatures dwelling in the Temple as they sing God's praises (verse 4).

A blessing is offered for pilgrims traveling to Zion. There is every assurance that they will be refreshed along the way, even on the passage through a usually arid valley, Baca. The psalmist then utters a prayer for Israel's king.

The last stanza of this popular psalm (verses 10-12) is one of the great gems of literature, a sparkling lyric poem of sheer sweetness. The *tents* of wickedness may be the homes of ungodly persons in the city from which this pilgrim has come. The *sun and shield* symbolize the strong defenses that God provides for those whose faith is strong. This lovely poem closes with a beatitude for persons who trust God.

Revive Us Again (Psalm 85)

The psalm opens with a stanza of praise and thanks for mercy and forgiveness and for relief from God's anger. The prayer is spoken in remembrance of some earlier occasion when Israel had repented and earned the blessing of God. It may have been the return from exile.

The second stanza (verses 4-7) reveals that the present generation's situation may be somewhat less serious than the one the psalmist remembers. Here the prayer is directed toward God's saving power, but there is no indication of wrath or disaster of the magnitude of the captivity.

In verse 8 the psalmist asks God to speak, fully assured that all is going to be well. The remaining verses (8*b*-13) are the psalmist's portrait of what the nation's religious experiences will be when God has answered the prayers of the faithful and made the divine presence a reality among them. It is an attractive picture of spiritual revival.

There Is None Like God (Psalm 86)

The psalmist has taken refuge in the Temple and addresses a prayer to God. The psalm is organized into three stanzas, the first of which deals with personal problems, chiefly poverty. Here is a godly person, a faithful servant filled with admiration for a gracious, loving, good God. Despite the personal circumstances, the psalmist has a happy, optimistic outlook. Verse 7 suggests that the relationships with God are secure enough to warrant an assumption that the prayers will be answered.

In the second stanza, the attention shifts toward God. Stature among the lesser gods, universal sovereignty among the nations, and other attributes are praised. The psalmist seeks information about the quality of life that God has ordained and, remembering a brush with death, offers thanks for deliverance.

The third stanza reveals another source of the psalmist's anxieties. Enemies are at hand bent on destruction. The psalmist pleads the case, asking pity from a God who gives every assurance of steadfast love for the faithful. The argument has an interesting twist at its conclusion. In verse 17 the psalmist suggests to God that, if divine assistance is forthcoming, it is certain to be noted by the enemies who then will feel a sense of shame.

The City of God (Psalm 87)

This short poem is a ritual song of Zion. It was the inspiration for the first line of John Newton's great hymn, *Glorious Things of Thee are Spoken, Zion City of Our God.* In stanza one the psalmist praises Zion as God's best-loved dwelling place of any in Israel *(Jacob).* Then God speaks in verse 4, mentioning the names of *those who acknowledge* (NIV) or *know* (NRSV) *me.* Among the names included is *Rahab,* a pseudonym for Egypt. Collectively the nations in the list are the present homeland of pilgrims who have come to Zion to celebrate one of the festivals. The meaning of verse 4*b* is obscure; we are unable to identify the antecedent of *This one.* The high point of the psalm occurs in verses 5-6. It is here that God may have been establishing the rights of citizenship in Zion for all Hebrews, regardless of their geographic origins. It has been suggested that the *register* of verse 6 is simply a roster of the nations. On the other hand, a God with loving concern for individuals would hardly have established Zion without some provision for the rights of individuals.

The singers and dancers of verse 7 rejoice, affirming that the joys of life and their own creative energies as performing artists are derived from God's loving presence in Zion.

Down to the Pit (Psalm 88)

Here is one of very few psalms that do not have a single note of hope. Of all this magnificent literature, this poem is the most sorrowful. It opens with the familiar cry for help. Day and night the psalmist utters the appeal. The recital of troubles is a sad monologue, beginning with verse 3. It is clear that death is at hand for this troubled soul whom God has apparently included among those soon to be dispatched to Sheol. The psalmist is convinced that alienation from God is complete and that there is no chance for salvation. This person's destiny is the deepest pit in all of the land of death (verses 5-7).

Just how loathsome the psalmist has become is made clear by the detail of verse 8. Moreover, being a prisoner has added to the repulsiveness. The questions in verses 10-12 are purely rhetorical. The psalmist already knows the answers. Those who are *dead* (NIV) are beyond God's love; the *shades* (NRSV) cannot ever rise from Sheol. Communication from the *Pit* (verse 4) is cut off completely.

Verse 13 is a reiteration of the appeal of verse 1. Because death does not yet have the upper hand, further prayer and supplication are offered. But sadly, the psalmist admits to feelings of terror, dread, and utter helplessness (verses 15-17). What seems worst of all is to have been abandoned to abject loneliness. None are there to console, and the curtain of eternal night seems to have fallen.

Broken Promises? (Psalm 89)

This psalm may be likened to a drama. It is divided into three acts, preceded by a prologue of praise. The historical era in which the psalm is set cannot be determined from the text. The prologue is clearly recounting some important history that would place the speaker at a date after the monarchy. Some observers have suggested the period of the captivity as likely.

Verses 5-18 portray God as maker and sustainer of the world. Within the celestial council the supreme being is God. The divine role in bringing the chaos under control and establishing the mountains is set forth (verses 9-12). Control of the seas is symbolized by the destruction of Rahab, fierce mythological creature of prehistoric waters of the deep. Perhaps more important in this drama of Israel's history is God's mighty act of instituting the principles of righteousness and justice (verse 14). The fact that God has revealed the divine nature by virtue of mighty acts is cause for exultation and praise (verses 15-17). A joyful assertion that both the people and the king belong to God (verse 18) closes the first act.

The second act is centered on history during the monarchy. It is chiefly David's covenant with God, the details of which are found in 2 Samuel 7:14-29. The anointing (verse 20) is described in Psalm 2. The language of these verses will be quite familiar to readers of the psalms of David. The *horn* of verse 24 is David's personal strength and valor. Verse 29 reaffirms God's promise to David that his lineage is established forever (Psalm 2:8).

The tone of act three makes this psalm a tragedy. Conditions favorable to Israel no longer exist. God has rejected the covenant with David, despite a promise not to lie (verse 35). Moreover, a king in David's lineage has been removed from the court, Jerusalem is in ruins, and Jews have been transported to Babylon for what is to be seventy years of captivity. The dethroned king is Jehoiachin (2 Kings 24:15-17). The loss of the crown, scepter, sword, and throne makes the sack of Jerusalem and the Exile seem terribly final (verses 39-45).

In desperation the psalmist turns to God with the plaintive *How Long, O Lord?* The language of these last few lines is like that of a dying person; it symbolizes the death of Israel which now seems to be a foregone conclusion. So final is it that the psalmist can do little but simply ask God to remember.

Verse 52 does not belong to this psalm. It is a beatitude that closes Book III of the Psalms.

§ § § § § § §

The Message of Psalms 81–89

With two exceptions, this group of psalms deals with sorrowful situations seeming to range from mild melancholy to absolute resignation. The volatility of human nature is set over against the equanimity and faithfulness of God. Yet even those divine traits are brought into question by the dire circumstances portrayed in these dramatic poems. The general theme of the message is that Israel must bear sorrow as a condition of its existence and perhaps even of its destiny. Yet Israel is never without hope.

§ Sorrow is the consequence of doubting God's capacity to act in human affairs.

§ Corruption among officials in the heavenly council causes sorrow on earth.

§ Sorrow has been the fate of Middle Eastern countries in constant conflict with each other.

§ Sorrow may inspire efforts to renew a right relationship with God.

§ Despite sorrow of the most abject kind, in the presence of God one can attain a lightened heart.

§ Some situations seem to produce a kind of sorrow that is totally devoid of hope.

§ Sorrow virtually devoid of hope because of unanswered prayer may be somewhat consoled by simply asking God to remember.

§ § § § § § §

Psalms 90–98

Introduction to These Psalms

These psalms are hymns of wonder, praise, and thanksgiving. Their lines are sources of inspiration to people everywhere. They are addressed to the Lord who reigns over all the earth. Some of the richest language in Christian hymnody and liturgy is derived from these psalms. Some of the great hymns of Christendom are based on the familiar texts of these psalms. Isaac Watts's "O God, Our Help in Ages Past" uses Psalm 90's majestic lines. With that psalm we open this part of the commentary.

A Heart of Wisdom (Psalm 90)

Literary critics have included the poetry of this psalm among the truly sublime classics of literature. It consists of two distinct parts. The first is a meditation (verses 1-12) on the contrasts between the human life span and God's eternity. The second part is a prayer (verses 13-17) for the constancy of God's love.

The psalmist begins by acknowledging God's infinite, eternal nature (verses 1-2). Verses 3-4 accent the differences between God and the people. The *dust* is, of course, mortality. Verse 3*b* is a complementary parallelism to verse 3*a*, accenting the limited human life span. Verse 4 is another word picture of the differences between God and humanity. God's control of the length of our days is the subject of a striking literary couplet (verses 5-65). The reasons for the limited length are given in the sentences that follow (verses 7-8). In verse 9, wrath is God's reaction to human tendencies toward the sins that limit our days.

The psalmist defines the life expectancy of people as seventy years, eighty if we are stronger, but then adds the realistic appraisal that they are surely years of trouble and are soon gone (verses 9-10). The *who* in the question of verse 11 may well be those who have learned to live in the fear of the Lord. They are the ones who may be taught to use each day wisely (verse 12).

The psalmist, recognizing the sinful nature of humanity, turns to the Lord pleading for pity. The hope is to be given some days of happiness as recompense for having suffered affliction. The prayer also petitions for a revelation of divine actions so that all might better know God's steadfast love and enduring power as the sovereign ruler (verse 16). The prayer ends with an appeal to God to favor Israel's people by making their daily work acceptable by divine standards.

God Is the Most High (Psalm 91)

The *Most High* was a name given to Israel's deity in the days following the establishment of the tribes. The polytheism of early settlers in Canaan influenced Israel's religious beliefs to the extent that gods of lesser stature than the *Most High* did exist. The *angels* of verse 11 were members of the councils of lesser deities we have found elsewhere in these psalms.

This psalm is a straightforward testimony of a person who has known the joys of intimate association with the *Most High* and for whom God is indeed a *refuge* (verses 1-2). Deliverance from the common enemies of disease and evil deeds of adversaries are happy manifestations of living under God's sheltering care. The evils in verses 5-6 are, in the traditions of early Israel, the work of demons who stalk the people of God day and night.

The psalmist is certain that trust in the goodness of God (dwelling in the *shelter of the Most High*) will keep one safe. The numbers of verse 7 are vivid imagery to emphasize the point. Immunity from the plague (*punishment*) is also promised (verse 8). Verses 9-10 reiterate the promises of the preceding stanzas.

In verses 11-12 the function of guardian angels is described. The animals (verse 13) symbolize enemies who can be readily vanquished by one who is secure in the Lord.

The final stanza finds God speaking about the faithful servant who is the subject of the preceding sentences. It is a divine declaration of confidence in persons in the community of faith and righteousness. In ritual, the words would be spoken by a priest as a benediction.

Thy Works Are Great (Psalm 92)

This is a liturgical hymn of joy appropriate to the sabbath. The first stanza is a call to worship with a sentence of gratitude for the elation of the moment. Adulation of God's good works (verse 5) is colored by a naive assumption that only brilliant people can comprehend divine actions (verse 6). All God's people can know good from evil and understand that the destiny of the wicked is death beneath the earth. On the other hand, God will live forever *exalted* (NIV) *on high* (NRSV).

In verses 10-11 the psalmist expresses unparalleled elation. The exalted *horn* is a symbol of strength and power. Anointment with oil is a symbol of wealth and social standing. Looking down on defeated enemies completes the picture of prosperous success.

The last stanza of the psalm equates prosperity with righteousness. The psalmist is eager to show that direct relationship with the metaphor of healthy, long-lived trees. While this equation is not in agreement with the experience of other psalmists who have discovered prosperity among the very wicked, there is an interesting moral that emerges. This psalmist would agree that the prosperity the righteous enjoy is, in fact, God's grace at work in the world.

God's Decrees Are Sure (Psalm 93)

This psalm is a declaration of God's everlasting kingship. It reinforces the intention of Israel to have no gods other than the one whose throne was *established from of old* (NRSV) or *long ago* (NIV) (verse 2). This is the same God whose power to tame the floods and bring order out of chaos caused the psalmist to sing with joy, *the LORD on high is mighty* (NIV) or *majestic on High is the LORD* (NRSV). Yet the power of the Lord is not limited to control of the physical universe. In a single line (verse 5), the power of the entire moral fabric of human society is exposed. God's decrees are sure.

Judge of the Earth (Psalm 94)

The psalm begins with a vigorous summons to the God of vengeance to come and judge the earth. In particular God is being asked to do something about wicked, arrogant sinners whose actions (verses 4-6) are simply beyond belief. What makes them even more offensive is their mockery of the Lord (verse 7).

At this point a stern lecture is delivered (verses 8-11) to these vile people. The God whom they have mocked as being unable to see them is, quite to the contrary, the God who knows all their thoughts. The God of Jacob (Israel) who created ears and eyes knows the thoughts of everyone. And that God who is both judge and teacher surely has knowledge useful for teaching (verse 10).

The psalmist continues the lecture with a blessing on those who willingly hear and obey the Lord's instruction (verses 12-15). The objective of that teaching is the disciplined life, together with the assurance that God will not abandon the people of the covenant. The promise of justice is also affirmed.

In the lines of the final stanza (verses 16-23) the

problems of a person falsely accused are discussed. Perhaps this section illustrates the special quality of God's interest in and care for individuals. The inquiry which opens this stanza evokes an immediate response: It was the Lord who stood against the wicked (verse 17), saving the psalmist's life. Several different circumstances (verses 18-19) have prompted similar responses from God. Is it possible that the wicked, evil tormentors are in league with God? Clearly this cannot be. The God who reigns above and who is the refuge of the righteous is also a God of vengeance. Surely *God will destroy them* (NIV) *wipe them out!* (NRSV)

Sing to the Lord (Psalm 95)

Two distinct sections comprise this great hymn of praise. The first section is a ritual of worship and the second is an oracle delivered by the Lord. This psalm would have been sung on the occasion of enthronement of the Lord as King and renewal of the covenant. The ritual begins with a joyous invitation to sing praises and thanksgiving (verses 1-2).

Praise continues into verse 3 followed by a vivid portrait of God the Creator (verses 4-5). It is a lovely echo of a part of the Creation story (Genesis 1:9-10). A second invitation to worship is more solemn, involving the acts of bowing and kneeling. It is the most sacred part of the ritual as worshipers are now in the intimate presence of God, presumably at the high altar (verses 6-7). The metaphors of shepherd and sheep are in keeping with the tenderness of the ceremony and the nature of God's loving care. As the worshipers are bowed, a soloist bids them listen to the word of God (verse 7c).

The remainder of the psalm is God's prophetic oracle, warning Israel that it must not behave as its ancestors did during the years of wandering in the wilderness. The episode at Meribah and Massah is recorded in Exodus 17:1-7. It is the sad story of rebellion despite the miracle of water springing from dry rocks. Because of this and other instances of defiance of God, the people endured punishment and death in the wilderness. That generation never got to the Promised Land—the *enter my rest* of verse 11.

Declare God's Glory (Psalm 96)

This hymn was written for the annual festival of enthronement of the Lord. The rites are a magnificent drama complete with full splendor and pageantry. The psalmist begins with a call to sing praises. The song is to be a *new song,* symbolic of the new year which is about to begin. All the world's peoples are included in the invitation. The intent of the praise is to announce the glorious deeds which Israel's God has performed (verse 3).

The psalmist pauses to remind the listeners that other gods of the people are merely idols without the character and depth of Israel's one God (verses 5-6). The call to ascription that follows (verses 7-8) is a summons to pledge obedience to Israel's God. It precedes the sacrificial offering which takes place in the inner courts of the Temple. Holy splendor (verse 9) suggests priestly vestments appropriate to that crucial part of the rites.

The climax of the psalm occurs in verse 10 when the lector announces the mystical enthronement. God is renewed as King, once again to rule as Creator, Sustainer, and Judge. The remainder of the psalm is joyous exultation. The whole world feels the magnetic presence of God. Bathed in divine radiance, all that is in the world sings for joy (verses 11-12). Essential to Israel's conception of humanity is the idea of justice—judgment with equity. God alone must be the final arbiter of justice. A fitting close to this psalm is the announcement that God will judge the earth.

Lord of All the Earth (Psalm 97)

This psalm, like the preceding one, is a hymn of enthronement, filled with vivid word pictures of what the reigning God is like (verse 1). Again the whole earth is summoned to praise. *Many coastlands* (NRSV) are the *distant lands* (NIV) beyond Israel's immediate neighbors; doubtless, all of the known world is intended. How is it that Israel's God is to be revealed to the coastlands? *Clouds and thick darkness* are symbolic of the fact that God is never really seen by people. Essential to the enthronement rites is the reaffirmation of Israel's belief that *righteousness and justice* originate with God (verse 2). *Fire* (verse 3) is the historic emblem of the brilliance and power of God's presence. Verses 4-5 remind the listeners that the physical *world* is not just God's creation, but changes can be made in it by the one who is about to be newly enthroned.

In the second stanza angels are introduced in order that they may proclaim God's glory. By means of their heavenly chorus, idol worshipers will be put to shame and all other lesser gods will be obliged to bow down. Zion, too, will hear their heavenly music causing the women of the Temple to be elated. The real reason for all the jubilation, however, is justice (verse 8c), an essential God has covenanted with Israel to manifest. The chorus concludes with stirring words of exultation.

The final verses are an oracle of counsel and encouragement to the righteous. They will experience light and joy if they live with upright hearts. Thanks be to God.

The Victory of Our God (Psalm 98)

This psalm is also a hymn of praise to be sung at the festival of the new year. It fits the form of a ritual poem, written for the annual ceremony of enthroning God as the sovereign King of the universe. The opening line is a call for the annual *new song,* symbolic of the process of renewing the covenant. The song need not be new but this celebrated occasion is always new.

The theme of the psalm is God's victory over unrighteousness, injustice, and the chaotic forces of the physical world. These evils were dealt with throughout the literature of the enthronement ritual, and their defeat contributed to the excitement surrounding the celebration.

Israel's claim that God is the universal sovereign is laid before the world (verse 2). The rescue of Israel is *vindication* (NRSV) or *salvation* (NIV) (proof) of God's mighty acts in history (verse 3).

Another vigorous call to worship comprises stanza two. The singing is to be accompanied by instrumental music. The *horn* (NRSV) is a shophar, a *ram's horn* (NIV), still in use during the Jewish new year celebrations.

In verses 7-8 the psalmist calls for additional praise. The whole world of nature rings with the music of God's creative presence. The last verse affirms again the essential character of God as the *judge* of the earth. It conforms to an essential belief of Jews and Christians alike that God is a God of justice.

§ § § § § § §

The Message of Psalms 90–98

The central theme of this cluster of psalms is the kingship of God. Four of these psalms (93; 96; 97; 98) are directly concerned with the enthronement ritual. The others have features about them that relate to the concept of God as the monarch, reigning over all the earth. Much of the literature is dramatic and written with imagination and high emotion. But the message is clear and decisive.

§ Israel's God is God above all gods.
§ Israel's God is the *Most High*.
§ Israel's God is a teacher of wisdom.
§ Israel's God is a God of the covenant.
§ Israel's God is utterly reliable.
§ Israel's God judges the peoples of the earth.
§ Israel's God created the world.
§ Israel's God is a God of victory.

§ § § § § § §

Psalms 99–106

Introduction to These Psalms

These psalms are lyric poetry dealing with praise, thanksgiving, and history. While some deep sorrow appears, the prevailing mood is joy and celebration. A predominant theme is that God endures. Time, in the vision of God, had no beginning and will have no end. To the people of Israel, the quality of timelessness was a beacon of hope. Just as God had brought them through their tumultuous history, as the poignant memories in the lines of these psalms reveal, so God will shepherd countless of their generations yet unborn. An enduring God to lean on gives Israel hope in the face of hostility.

Holy Is the Lord (Psalm 99)
This psalm is another in the series of hymns written to celebrate the new year festival and the annual enthronement of the Lord. The ritual begins with a familiar pronouncement of the Lord's sovereignty. God is in the Temple on Zion, seated on a throne supported by elaborately carved angelic figures. Their presence symbolizes the heavenly council. Eloquent versicles of praise are sung (verses 2-3) concluding with the acknowledgment of God's holiness. *Holy* in this context clearly distinguishes the Lord from any human personality and emphasizes purity and perfection as well as divinity.

In verse 4 the psalmist addresses God directly as the administrator of justice. There follows a short call to worship. The *footstool* (verse 5) may be the ark of the covenant situated just below God's earthly throne. The holiness refrain (verse 3) is repeated here.

Brief recollections of history are features of many ritual psalms. Here in verses 6-7 are memories of priestly persons of Israel's past whose special relationships with God cast them into the role of intercessors, arbitrators, and mediators. The *pillar of cloud* denotes the presence of an otherwise invisible God.

In verses 8-9 the psalmist recalls the dialogues between God and the priestly ones as well as the vengeance which they sustained. Repetition of the refrain of verses 3 and 5 closes this ritual hymn. Zion is the *holy mountain;*

Make a Joyful Noise (Psalm 100)

People of all creeds, generation after generation, have treasured these beautiful sentences as their entrance into the vital experiences of sacred worship. The theme of this beloved liturgical poem is God's faithfulness and enduring, steadfast love. These majestic lines show how the characteristics of faithfulness and love foster the deepest gratitude in the hearts of the people.

Following the call to worship (verses 1-2), the psalmist sings a song of wisdom (verse 3). It reminds us that God is God above all other gods, that God created us, and that God cares for us as the shepherd cares for the sheep. These concepts are in the bedrock of Israel's religion.

Verse 4 is a ritual invitation to enter the inner precincts of the Temple to experience the actual presence of God. There, praise and thanksgiving may seem more personal. The second song of wisdom (verse 5) centers on God's enduring goodness, faithfulness, and constant love.

Loyalty or Love and Justice (Psalm 101)

This psalm is ascribed to David. Presumably it is his coronation pledge, somewhat like an oath of office and brief inaugural address. The central theme is a list of principles by which David will govern his private life as well as the responsibilities as sovereign. The words are a nearly perfect ideal of what a person in a position of leadership ought to be. The opening line sets the tone for what is to follow. It proclaims that *loyalty to* (NRSV) or *love of* (NIV) God will be uppermost in this kingship, an important responsibility of which is to administer divinely ordered justice. David agrees to this with gladness of heart. To be able to do this, the king must be without fault (verse 2). In a dramatic aside (verse 2b), the king sings an appeal for a closer, more intimate relationship with God.

The remainder of the poetry is a plainly stated code of ethics. Personal qualifications for leadership comprise verses 3-5. The inclusion of arrogance (verse 5) seems especially perceptive for a king. In verse 6 the king makes it clear that the servants of government will be chosen from among the ranks of people faithful to God. Furthermore, shady dealings and false witness will not be tolerated (verse 7). Verse 8 is the king's threat that the practitioners of evil will be denied admission to Zion.

Enthroned Forever (Psalm 102)

As noted earlier, deep sorrow is depicted. It is here in this poem of extraordinary personal distress. The psalmist is in isolation because of some deadly malady. Using the common literary structure of the lament, the psalmist begins with the cry for help. It is followed by a comprehensive account of the problems (verses 3-11). The imagery is as vivid and imaginative as one encounters in any of the psalms. The picture is one of devastating physical and mental torture.

Despite the gravity of the situation, the psalmist is able to forget his tribulation long enough to offer a prophetic oracle (verses 17-18). An acknowledgment of God's enduring timelessness opens the prophecy. Zion will be restored and God will reappear in glory and will care for the poor. The time for deliverance is at hand. The text of the oracle does not indicate a specific episode. The psalmist may have been thinking about the possibility of release from the Babylonian captivity. In verse 18 a request that someone make a record is noted. We do not know what the antecedent of *this* is. It may be the preceding oracle or the one that follows. The psalmist's oracle in verses 19-22 is obviously oriented toward future generations. The choice of words shows the psalmist to have been familiar with prophetic writings. Its noble purpose is made clear in verse 21.

Now the psalmist abruptly returns to the lament. Blame for the sorrowful circumstances is ascribed to God (verse 23). Why would God strike down a person in middle years, especially a God whose years endure?

The subject of that enduring quality is developed further in the last stanza. With profound insight the psalmist observes that the whole earth itself will perish, but God will endure through years that have no end. A personal note of sorrow closes this bittersweet song (verse 28). The dying psalmist holds dearly to the hope that the children of the family will be secure in God's keeping.

Blessed Be the Lord (Psalm 103)

This psalm is one of the great masterpieces of world literature. It is a song of thanksgiving, sung by an individual of deep spiritual insight. The author is assumed to be David, although different opinions exist in the scholarly community. Yet only a person with the intellectual stature and artistic creativity of someone like David could have written such a magnificent testimony.

A beatitude sung as a call to praise opens the psalm. It is addressed inwardly rather than to a group and expresses gratitude for God's fulfillment of every need (verses 1-5).

The psalmist then sings a longer stanza of praise and thanksgiving (verses 6-18). Its verses are among the more memorable in the Psalter. They are addressed to the congregation as reminders of God's generosity and goodness to Israel. God's attributes of grace, mercy, and steadfast love are described by the most quotable phrases of incomparable beauty. The ideas appearing in some of the lines seem remarkably similar to New Testament expressions. Verses 10 and 12 read much like some Christian definitions of the gifts of grace and forgiveness. As noted above in the introduction to this part of the Psalter, the general theme is the enduring nature of God. In verses 15-18 it is contrasted to the transitory condition of humanity in lines of exquisite grace. Imagine the countless numbers of God's people who have achieved serenity in the face of death with the companionship of these words.

In the final stanza the psalmist returns to the literary style of the beatitude. The scope of the blessings is all-encompassing. It ranges from the council of heaven to the servant world of humanity to everything in creation and even to the depths of a human soul (verse 22).

God's Creation (Psalm 104)

This is one of the nature psalms, written in somewhat greater detail than Psalms 8 and 19. Its intent is to praise God as one who created the earth but who stands above and beyond it as an eternal being. The descriptions of God's acts in the creation of the earth and its physical features are tinged with the mythology of the Babylonians and probably Canaanite neighbors (verses 2-4). The greater descriptive realism which follows (verses 5-23) is remarkably insightful. Imagine the patient observation that must have been required to have been able to describe so much of nature so accurately. The lyrical quality of the poetry only serves to enhance interest in the more scientific information.

As the psalm moves on, the psalmist seems overcome with all of creation that is to be included in these descriptions. And then follows a joyous stanza of praise to the Lord. The psalmist is evidently standing on the bluffs overlooking the Mediterranean Sea. Ships of the coastal peoples are in view as is a whale *(Leviathan)*. The *Leviathan* was also a monster of Canaanite mythology, but this psalmist is too much of a realist to report that a seven-headed monster has been seen in the nearby sea.

The conversation with the Lord continues as the psalmist describes the effect of the changing seasons (verses 27-30). The gardens, orchards, and fields respond to God's control by flourishing during the summer growing season and dying back when God's face is hidden (winter). The psalmist is impressed with the miracle of renewal every spring (verse 30).

The majority of nature, which the psalmist obviously has studied carefully and has now sung about, has stimulated further words of praise (verses 31-34). The whole earth is full of the glory of God's works. Glory endures forever and is worthy of lifelong praise. The denunciation of sinners (verse 35) seems almost an afterthought, with no particular relevance to the lines preceding it.

How God Saved Israel (Psalm 105)

Here is an account of God's mighty deeds recorded in Israel's history. The listeners are to celebrate the glory of God's name. They are also asked to remember the wonderful works as evidence of God's continuous presence with Israel. The remainder of the psalm is a catalogue of *miracles, judgments,* and *wonderful works* (NRSV) or *wonders* (NIV) as noted in verse 5. These verses trace the history of Israel from the covenant with Abraham through the patriarchs to Joseph and the enslavement in Egypt (verses 8-25). The appointment of Moses and Aaron to leadership positions is also recorded (verses 26-27). The miracles in Egypt are noted in some detail (verses 28-36). Additional mighty deeds included in this brief history are the deliverance from the hand of

Pharaoh, the Exodus, and the wilderness experiences (verses 37-42). The final stanza (verses 43-45) records the paramount event in the early history of Israel's people. The hand of God led them out of the wilderness to Canaan, where *they fell heir* (NIV) *took possession* (NRSV).

National Guilt (Psalm 106)

This psalm, like the preceding, is an account of Israel's history. However, unlike Psalm 105 which features the saving acts of God, this psalm addresses the sins and human error which have loomed large in Israel's alienations from God. The record is one of frequent rebellion.

The psalm opens with a stanza of praise and thanksgiving for God's enduring, steadfast love and mighty acts. The just are also remembered with a beatitude (verse 3). A cry for help follows from a person who wants a better economic position (verses 4-5). The request seems to have little if any relevance to the streams of thought about national sin which are the subjects of verses to follow.

In verse 6 the tone is set for the recital of the record of national guilt. The rebellion at the Red Sea (Exodus 14:10-12) is the first on the list (verses 7-12). Israel, refusing to trust God, elected to stay in Egypt and serve other gods. However, God's saving grace got them through the sea and into the wilderness and then they believed for a while. The second instance (verses 13-15) was a rebellion in the desert. (See Numbers 11:4-20.)

Another entry in this record of sin is the uprising of the princes against Moses and Aaron. It is the subject of Numbers 16. The well-known story of the golden calf (verses 19-23) is told in Exodus 32:1-6.

Verses 24-27 describe the rejection of God's counsel that they should migrate to the Promised Land. Their lack of courage incurred God's anger. (See the account of this episode in Numbers 14:1-12. (The next occurrence (verses 28-31) is the worship of Canaanite gods during the encampment across the Jordan River from Jericho. Violation of the first commandment was associated with other evils. The full story is told in Numbers 25.

Verses 32-33 are a flashback to an episode that took place early in the wilderness trek. It is discussed in this commentary in connection with Psalm 81. Verses 34-39 describe the sin after the settlement of Israel in Canaan. God's instructions were to avoid cultural mixing with the Canaanites. Israel failed, and the integrity of her national heritage was compromised. (See Deuteronomy 7:1-11.)

The final entry in this tragic record (verses 40-46) is an overview of the pattern of rebellion, faithlessness, and apostasy. It is a saga of the cycle of sin, repentance, forgiveness, and deliverance. That God has redeemed Israel again and again shows God's enduring, steadfast love.

How often has Israel raised her voice to cry for salvation (verse 47)? And how often has God responded? The story is a glorious one of God's complete faithfulness. Verse 48a is a beatitude to God for being the *God of Israel* forever. The last lines (verse 48b) are a doxology for Book IV of the Psalms.

§ § § § § § §

The Message of Psalms 99–106

One recurrent theme in these psalms is the enduring faithfulness of God. A second theme is the reverence Israel feels, deep within its national character, for the integrity of the covenants made with God. Despite their repeated failures, these people have never permanently rejected the outstretched hand of God. Perhaps this is because God is everlasting and unchangeable, the refuge to which the people may return again and again.

§ God's steadfast love endures forever.
§ God's justice is everlasting.
§ God's grace, mercy, and faithfulness endure forever.
§ God is King forever.
§ God will keep a covenant with Israel forever.

§ § § § § § §

Psalms 107–114

Introduction to These Psalms

The basic credo of Socrates, the intellectual giant of
early Greek philosophy, was to live well. This meant
living in accord with truth. Living well in the tradition of
Israel's covenant relationship with God is to live
righteously. The general theme addressed in this group
of psalms is advice on the art of living righteously.

God Fills the Hungry (Psalm 107)

Two distinct sections comprise this psalm. The first is a
compilation of stories of deliverance. Each of the several
cases deals with persons who have encountered
difficulties of varying sorts. In each instance, a cry for
help is addressed to God and the result is rescue from
travail and restitution of prosperity and the good life. A
word of thanksgiving closes each story. The principals in
these little dramas are the *redeemed* of verse 2.

The first story is found in verses 4-9. Desert wanderers
are desperately hungry and thirsty. A cry to the Lord
brings deliverance in the form of a new life in a city.
Those who have been filled are requested to thank the
Lord (verse 8) for the good things that have been done.

The second story (verses 10-16) describes prisoners
who have defied God. Hard labor was a traditional
punishment for hardened criminals. The cry to God
brought deliverance. Those who were released are asked
to thank God with a repetition of verse 8.

The third story (verses 17-22) is the familiar syndrome

of incurable disease. Israel's early beliefs held disease to be the result of sin (verse 17). These persons are critically ill and waiting for death. Their cry for help brings deliverance. The psalmist urges them to thank God.

The fourth story (verses 23-32) is that of the historic plight of seafaring people. In the midst of a raging storm and threatened with death by drowning, the sailors cry to God. Their delivery is accomplished and the psalmist bids them to thank the Lord as verse 8 is repeated.

The turning point in these short stories with happy endings is the earnest cry for help. God responds positively, not just because of the cry, but because of fundamental changes in the spiritual condition of those in trouble. Change has allowed an honest self-recognition of sin and forced a firm decision to avoid it. The final step in this experience is the decision to trust God completely.

The latter section of this psalm (verses 33-43) seems to summarize what God has accomplished in the lives of the repentant sinners of the stories in section one. But it also addresses more generally what God does for the people as a matter of faithfulness. The special care for the oppressed, the support of the faithful who are the producers of the community's food supply, and the feeding of the hungry are examples from the psalmist's experience. They are all manifestations of God's steadfast love.

A Steadfast Heart (Psalm 108)

This psalm duplicates segments of two other psalms. See the commentary on the psalms as indicated. Verses 1-5 are identical to Psalm 57:7-11. The lines are a magnificent hymn of praise. Verses 6-13 replicate Psalm 60:5-12. Those verses are an ancient oracle reminding Israel that God once gave them the land of Canaan.

False Accusations (Psalm 109)

Forty psalms deal in one way or another with false accusations. The persistence of the problem in Israelite society may explain the critical position that justice came to occupy among the attributes of God. The problem may also have accounted in part for the establishment of a fairly extensive system of judicial administration.

In this psalm a victim of malicious lying enters the sanctuary to pray that God will speak in his defense. The prayer (verses 1-5) is brief and to the point. Returning good for evil has failed to stem the tide of falsehoods.

In most of the false-accusation psalms the opening prayer is followed by a petition for assistance. This psalm differs by having inserted at this point (verses 6-19) a lengthy account of the curses which have been delivered against this poor psalmist. The actual charges are recounted in verses 16-18. When this frightening recitation is ended a tersely worded but comprehensive petition is offered (verses 20-21). The psalmist begs that the curses the accusers have invoked will, in turn, become their just deserts and, further, that deliverance will be forthcoming because of *steadfast love* (NRSV) or *goodness of your love* (NIV) and for the *sake* of God's good *name*. The good name here includes the revealed power of God that assures justice with equity. Implied in these lines is the presumption of the psalmist's innocence.

In most of the psalms of the falsely accused, the petition is accompanied by a description of the psalmist's present condition. The poverty, sickness, and scorn manifest in verses 22-25 mean that this psalmist is no exception.

A more vigorous petition is offered (verses 26-29), made up largely of curses on the accusers. The psalmist then promises to give great thanks, assuming that the God who is always ready to help the falsely accused will judge this poor wretched person to be innocent.

At God's Right Hand (Psalm 110)

This psalm was written for use during the coronation of a king. In Israel's religious practices the anointed king was invited to sit at God's right hand.

As the psalm begins, God is speaking to the king. In practice, the voice of God is heard through a high priest. The *footstool* of verse 1 is an expression that may have originated with a Babylonian illustration of a king with one foot on the neck of an enemy. The *scepter* of verse 2 is the symbol of kingly authority. Authority is enhanced if the Lord has committed it to the king as a part of the coronation ritual.

Verses 2-3 are an oracle extending the king's rule from Jerusalem to the borders of the nation. God gives assurance that the people will volunteer themselves to join the king in battle. The king will be restored in vigor daily just as *dew* appears every morning.

The oracle continues in verse 4 as God vows faithfulness to the promises made to Abram. The *order of Melchizedek* is a guild of kings established when Abram entered Jerusalem after the rescue of Lot (Genesis 14:14-20).

In the final stanza (verses 5-7) the priest-psalmist sings an oracle foretelling God's mighty deeds when Israel goes to war. The king will be victorious because God is a God of justice; the pagan kings will be destroyed. The *he* of verse 7 is evidently the king. The *brook* (NIV) or *stream* (NRSV) may be a place in the valley of Kidron where Solomon was anointed king. The episode is described in 1 Kings 1:28-40.

God Redeems the Nation (Psalm 111)

This psalm is considered by literary critics to be another of the masterworks of the Psalter. It appears in print as a single stanza of thoughtful praise to God for the redemption of Israel. A psalmist, addressing the congregation, opens the psalm with a great hallelujah. It is followed by enthusiastic words of thanks. Verses 2-9 constitute the main body of the text in which the psalmist dwells on the familiar theological themes that are the theophany, God's self-revelation. (See commentary on Psalm 50.) Power, justice, majesty, moral law *(precepts)*, and faithfulness, all manifestations of the deity, are included.

Verse 9 recounts the *redemption* of Israel. God's mighty acts have saved Israel many times and in ways that cause the enemies to regard her God with terror *(fear)*.

With the *fear of the* LORD in mind, the psalmist utters one of the more memorable *wisdom* verses in the entire Psalter (verse 10). What better advice for the righteous!

Blessed Generosity (Psalm 112)

This psalm closely parallels Psalm 1 in form and content. Its literary style suggests that it was written by the author of Psalm 111. The content provides a catalogue of benefits which accrue to the righteous. We discover that a generous God is responsible.

As the psalm opens, a hallelujah is sounded and a beatitude is spoken for one who *fears the* LORD. The person who greatly delights in the commandments is one who not only keeps them but has a special interest in quiet meditation and thoughtful contemplation about them. Imagine the benefits such a person would derive (verses 2-3). Not the least important of the benefits is God's light shed on the study, increasing substantially one's fund of knowledge and understanding (verse 4*a*).

In verse 4*b* the psalmist calls attention to three of God's attributes. The line does not seem to be directly related either to the preceding or to the following verse. Perhaps it is simply an enthusiastic reminder to the congregation of the richness of God's personality. In verse 5 another blessing is given. *It is well* (NRSV; NIV=*good*) is a variation of the use of *blessed* or *happy* to begin a beatitude. The benefits of dealing justly and generously with people are enumerated in verses 6-9. But what about the wicked? How thoughtful of the psalmist to have included an accurate portrayal of the consequences of envy (verse 10).

God Lifts the Needy (Psalm 113)

Another of God's characteristics is the abiding concern for the poverty-stricken of this world. In this psalm the tender affection for the oppressed of the world is set over against the majestic power and grandeur of an omnipotent God of the whole universe. That such a deity could minister personally to the least of the world's people is incomprehensible to those who do not know Israel's God. The contrast gives the poetry its special value.

The initial hallelujah sets the mood for the stanza of exultation and praise to follow. *Servants* of verse 1 are the faithful who have gathered for worship. They are there to hear advice about care for the needy. As the blessing for the Lord is delivered, the psalmist takes care to profess that the *glory* of Israel's God is beyond that of the hearers. The intention is to develop the impression in the minds of the listeners that God is a full, superlative being. And with that assertion (verse 4) the stage is carefully set for developing the most vivid of contrasts.

In verse 5, God is portrayed occupying a place in the highest heights and, from that exalted position, reaching down to lift the poor. To strengthen and dramatize this vivid portrait of a generous, loving God, the psalmist includes the divinely inspired feast of prince and pauper as well as the traditional support of widows and orphans. What better advice to the righteous than the wonderful example of an exalted God caring for people in want!

Historic Moments (Psalm 114)

This beautifully poetic literary gem is one of six psalms that Judaism identifies as the *Hallel*. The Hallel (Psalms 113-118) is recited during the celebration of Passover, commemorating the miracle in the last hours before the escape from Egypt (Exodus 12:3-36). The opening lines are vivid recollections of the flight from Egypt. Verse 2 is a memory of events forty years later at the conclusion of the wilderness trek. The destination was Canaan.

Verses 3-6 are written with the loveliest of metaphors and similes. It is not unusual in the literature of the Middle East to personify non-living objects and geologic and geographic events. The poetic descriptions of verses 3-4 become rhetorical questions in verses 5-6. The poet is affirming God's mighty acts to be well beyond the natural power of the divine Creation.

In the last two verses, the psalmist calls upon the whole earth to respond to almighty power represented by the *presence* of God (verse 7). *Tremble* might be variously interpreted as an earthquake in progress, or perhaps only shock waves of sound as thunder rolls across the landscape. Some translations use *dance,* suggesting symbolism for movements of the waters and the earth. The literary quality of this psalm, like Psalm 23, ought to stimulate readers to commit it to memory.

§ § § § § § §

The Message of Psalms 107–114

The psalms in this group are upbeat, poetically attractive, and filled with the earthly manifestation of Israel's generous God. The general theme of sound advice for righteous people is explicit in most of these psalms. Where it is not so evident, the characteristics of God may well serve as models of behavior.

§ A formula for living well is to admit one's sin, resolve to avoid it, and trust in God.
§ God cares for the hungry and we must do the same.
§ God sustains the righteous who may be falsely accused of criminal activity.
§ *The fear of the* LORD is the beginning of wisdom.
§ We benefit from dealing justly with others.
§ Benefits result from diligent study; God sheds light on our study of the ways of the Lord.
§ A God of extraordinary majesty and power ministers to the oppressed. Can righteous people do less?

§ § § § § § §

Introduction to These Psalms

The psalms in this part reveal deep feelings of genuine appreciation for God's gifts. The bounty is unlimited and of unusual variety. Israel's survival as a political presence in the world is understood to be the consequence of God's consistent intercession across centuries of turmoil.

God Is in the Heavens (Psalm 115)

In periods of national disaster Israel's condition was commonly that of deep humiliation. Particularly disconcerting were the taunts of pagan neighbors. Especially was this so when the God of Israel was being ridiculed for apparent impotence while the nation floundered helplessly. Despite the disastrous intervals, the prevailing mood throughout Israel's history was generally one of confidence and trust. In the light of that outlook, the arguments in this psalm are not surprising. The pagan's question in verse 2b stimulates a spirited response downgrading the pagan idols who simply can't compare with God (verses 3-8).

In verses 9-11, the psalmist appeals to Israel, to Aaron's priestly descendants, and to the Temple congregation to *trust in the* LORD. Why? Because the Lord has been and will continue to be good to them (verses 12-13). At this point in the ritual a priest pronounces a benediction (verses 14-15). The final stanza is a word picture of the universe as the people of Israel understood it. The *heavens* belong to God. The *earth* is for use as a habitation by the people, and Sheol is a land of *silence* for the dead who do not praise God. Because God is in the heavens and has promised Israel a heritage of generations without number, Israel can declare that the nation will live forever (verse 18).

God Hears a Prayer (Psalm 116)

This psalm is a personal testimony of what God did to relieve suffering and provide restoration. The psalmist was on the brink of death. From the depths of an anguished soul came a call for salvation (verses 3-4).

A prompt and positive response by the Lord (verse 2a) restored the dying psalmist to health. Deep gratitude is evident in the declaration of love with which the psalm opens. The psalmist adds more words extolling God's virtues, especially the care for the simple, common people of the Israelite society (verse 6). In verses 8-11, faith in God's ability to save lives is vigorously championed, whereas any hope placed in human efforts is futile.

In the latter portions of this psalm, the writer confronts the question of how to repay the Lord (verse 16). Paying one's vows to God must be accomplished in the presence of the congregation (verses 14, 18). Payments includes ritual obligations which must of necessity be performed. The *cup of salvation* (verse 13) is symbolic of sacrifice. A sacrifice of thanksgiving (freewill offering) is tendered (verse 17). Then follows the acknowledgment that it was God who saved the life of this person, the son of a faithful woman. In the end the psalmist praises God. The vows have been paid (spoken) in the beautiful environment of God's house. *Praise the LORD!*

All Nations Praise God (Psalm 117)

Here is a stirring hymn with which a service of worship is begun. It praises the power of God which supports divine sovereignty over all the nations of the world. The psalm also lauds God's *steadfast love* (NRSV) or *great love* (NIV) which again and again was given with saving grace to heal the crises in Israel's history. The absolute certainty of God's responses to Israel is evidence of faithfulness. *Praise the LORD!*

An Abundance of Gifts (Psalm 118)

This poem is a Hallel psalm sung at the Feast of the Passover. It has also found its way into Christian liturgy, particularly the Easter celebrations. Allusions to the New Testament story give the poem a prophetic tone.

The liturgy begins with an invitation to thank the Lord for the enduring gift of steadfast *love* (verse 1). The invitation is repeated for emphasis (verses 2-4).

The next three stanzas are Israel's great hymn of gratitude for centuries of protection from neighboring enemy nations. The psalmist is personifying the national experiences of righteousness and calamity. Verses 5-9 tell of the gladsome admission that Israel's confidence is in the Lord. In the following five verses (10-14) noisy military assaults on Israel are recounted. Despite the apparent size of the enemies' forces (verse 11), Israel prevailed. Their numbers are likened to swarms of *bees* but with God's help they were *cut off*. The simile of a fire of thorns means that enemies were overcome quickly in the same way that fire consumes the dry, brittle twigs of the thornbush.

In verses 15-18 the psalmist recalls thrilling days when Israel could be elated with the sense of victory. The metaphor of *the right hand* is in liberal use throughout the Scripture. It is symbolic of power and energy enabling God to vanquish Israel's foes. Because Israel can rely on the *right hand* of God, it will *live* forever, its precious memories including the deeds of a valiant God.

At the conclusion of this majestic hymn, the psalmist calls to the Temple guard to open the gates of righteousness. This bit of pageantry symbolizes admission into the glorious presence of God (verses 19-20).

The topic in the next stanza (verses 21-25) is God's redemption of Israel. Having faced frequent rejection,

Israel is elated to be the *building stone,* literally the master builder's keystone in the edifice of nations. The *day which the* LORD *has made* is a day of national celebration. Some interpreters of psalms have noted how readily the metaphor of the once-rejected building stone might be construed to symbolize Jesus Christ. A similar inference suggests that the *day* of verse 24 is Easter.

In verse 26 the psalmist blesses the congregation and proclaims the lordship of God. The *light* (verse 27b) God has provided probably means the wisdom of God's moral precepts. For the Christian, that *light* is clearly God's gift, *the light of the world,* Jesus Christ. The remainder of verse 27 is a description of the ancient practice of bearing to the altar the carcasses of sacrificial animals bound with supple tree branches. The altar had carved horns at the four corners. The psalm is brought to a close with verses of thanksgiving, verse 29 being a repetition of verse 1.

God's Moral Law (Psalm 119)

The uniqueness of this psalm is not just its extraordinary length. It is the most uniformly structured of any of the psalms with twenty-two stanzas of eight verses each. The literary format is that of an acrostic poem. All twenty-two letters of the Hebrew alphabet are used to form the acrostic. The initial letter of the first word in each line of a stanza is the same. In the first stanza of the psalm, the first letter of the Hebrew alphabet is used. The pattern is repeated stanza by stanza using the remaining twenty-one letters in alphabetic order. The acrostic format has no religious significance; it is simply a literary exercise. Several other acrostic psalms have been constructed (9; 10; 25; 34; 37; 111; 112; 145). The acrostic format of most of these is not as clear as that of Psalm 119. Editors' rearrangements and fragmented manuscripts in the compilation of the Psalter have doubtless distorted the acrostic structure of the original poems.

Psalm 119 is a treatise on law, particularly moral law. Because it is God's law divinely inspired and divinely created, it is perfect, absolute, and eternal.

In a psalm of this length, repetition of ideas is common and most of the situations described here are encountered in other psalms. For these reasons (and space limitations) commentary will be limited to the central theme of each stanza as it relates to God's gift of the law.

Verses 1-8: The central theme is a prayer that the psalmist's devotion to the law will be steadfast. Synonyms for the moral law appearing in this stanza are way, testimonies, precepts, statutes, commandments, ordinances.

Verses 9-16: Moral guidance for youth requires memorization of the law (*word* of verse 11) as well as diligent study of the Lord's statutes. *Word* (verse 9) is another synonym of moral law.

Verses 17-24: The *stranger* (NIV) or *alien* (NRSV) of this stanza is a finite being, troubled by enemies and falsely accused. God hears a petition for mercies and a promise of steadfastness to the law.

Verses 25-32: Death seems imminent and the will to live is fading (verse 28*a*). The psalmist pleads for strength to remain faithful and to continue to learn God's *precepts.*

Verses 33-40: The verses in this stanza repeat the single theme of an appeal to God to be a teacher of the law. Words of prayer solicit courage to resist temptations.

Verses 41-48: Personal benefits deriving from the existence of God's law include liberty (verse 45) and courage to speak before those who ridicule (verse 42) as well as those who are *kings* (verse 46).

Verses 49-56: The very thought of the *ancient law* (NIV) *ordinances* (NRSV) gives the psalmist both comfort and a singing heart (verse 54), despite affliction and public ridicule.

Verses 57-64: Study of the law has stimulated the psalmist to keep God's commandments (verse 60). Among the psalmist's friends who also love the law, a companionship has formed.

Verses 65-72: Knowledge and respect for the law have given the psalmist new life, despite his physical affliction. Persons with limited intellect (whole hearts) are slandering the psalmist, but love of the law grants immunity.

Verses 73-80: An afflicted psalmist prays for God's *comfort* and *mercy* and for oppressors to be forestalled. The psalmist's love of the law is a wonderful example for others despite the heartache.

Verses 81-88: The psalmist, a victim of violent persecution, prays for salvation, assuring God of loyalty and profound respect for the law.

Verses 89-96: If God's absolute *(fixed)* laws had not been available for study, this afflicted psalmist would surely have perished. Nothing else has the perfection of these laws.

Verses 97-104: Because of intense love of the law as well as faithful study and diligent meditation, the psalmist has achieved wisdom far beyond that of many others.

Verses 105-112: The law is a *lamp* and *light* for the psalmist. Despite misfortune and persecution, loyalty to God's *righteous ordinances* (NRSV) or *laws* (NIV) (verse 106) is faithfully promised.

Verses 113-120: The psalmist is struggling against practitioners of deceit and evil. A prayer is offered for strength to resist so that the law may be honored.

Verses 121-128: The psalmist prays for the security of God's presence and for *understanding* (NRSV) or *discernment* (NIV) *of statutes* (NIV) or *decrees* (NRSV).

Verses 129-136: Interpretations of the law are important. Yet there is sadness because people do not obey it.

Verses 137-144: God's law is not simply a catalogue of precepts administered at will. The law is God's essential presence revealed to Israel.

Verses 145-152: The psalmist begs for relief from persecution so that the law may be more readily obeyed.

Verses 153-160: The psalmist pleads for life on the grounds of loyalty to the law and disdain for the *faithless.*

Verses 161-168: Despite intense persecution, the psalmist continues to praise God for the gift of the law.

Verses 169-176: The psalmist pleads for deliverance. If

it is granted, a flood of *praise* will follow as will joyful attention to the moral *precepts* of God.

Woe Is Me (Psalm 120)

These lines in the psalm are the musings of a weary pilgrim who has traveled far from home. During these travels, the wanderer has encountered lying, deceitful people. Their weapons are death-dealing *arrows* and the embers of the burning *broom tree*, the wood of which yields a hot, long-lasting fire (verse 4).

At this point a deep melancholia has overcome the pilgrim (verse 5). Meshech is in Asia Minor between the Black and Caspian Seas, far from Israel. Thus the reference may be only symbolic. Kedar is closer to home. It is desert land on the southern border of Syria. The source of this psalmist's distress is the subject of verses 6-7. A peace-loving citizen of Israel is forced to dwell among warmongers.

I Lift Up My Eyes (Psalm 121)

This psalm is among the best-loved of the entire Psalter. Within the cultural inheritance of all humanity there is an attachment to the *hills,* places to which we repair for refreshment and renewal. But the psalmist professes a dependence on the Lord for *help* and, in the remainder of the psalm, provides several reasons why.

In verse 1 the psalmist may have been speaking of the hills of Jerusalem, perhaps Mount Zion. The psalmist's confidence is in God, the Creator. The *shade* in verse 5 is protection against the blazing middle-eastern sun. The potential harm from both the sun and the moon is a remnant of pre-Israelite mythology.

The final stanza professes trust and confidence. The psalmist proclaims that God's constant watchfulness is a precious gift.

A Prayer for Peace (Psalm 122)

This poem was recited by a pilgrim who has come to Jerusalem and is deeply impressed by what he has seen.

After perhaps a week in the city to participate in one of the festivals, the pilgrim is preparing to leave. The psalm consists of reflections about the experience.

In verse 1 the pilgrim speaks of the joy of worship in the Temple. The remainder of the psalm is a tribute to the city. Unity of the city is made possible by the proximity of Zion and the presence of God and by the periodic visits of tribal representatives according to a decree (verse 4). (See Deuteronomy 16:16-17.) The pilgrim recalls that David established Jerusalem as the capital city and God came to abide there also (2 Samuel 5:6-10).

The pilgrim invites the listeners to pray for peace in the city (verses 6-8). Overcome with joy, the pilgrim promises to seek good things for this beloved place (verse 9).

§ § § § § § §

The Message of Psalms 115–122

Throughout the commentary on these psalms, the emphasis is placed on the inexhaustible supply of riches which God makes available to Israel. Material wealth was conspicuously absent from Israel's needs. Their concerns went far deeper into spiritual hunger which God ably satisfied. With one exception (Psalm 120), the psalms in this group describe some magnificent gifts.

§ God has given the earth for the people to use.
§ God gives physical and spiritual health to the people.
§ God gives military victories to Israel.
§ God gives the keystone of the Kingdom to the world.
§ God gives light to a world in darkness.
§ God gives moral law to society.
§ God gives grace, mercy, and steadfast love.
§ God gives people the capacity to trust.

§ § § § § § §

Psalms 123–130

Introduction to These Psalms

The psalms in this part are lovely songs of trust and confidence. The ultimate consequence of complete trust and confidence is hope. Even when Israel was in the midst of disasters, the capacity to hope enabled the nation to reject the irrational behavior of despair. A most appealing statement of trust is found in Paul's letter to the Romans: *If God is for us, who is against us?* That question is a fitting introduction to a cluster of short poems which stress an intimate affiliation with God's gift of hope.

Enough of Contempt (Psalm 123)

This psalm is a brief but poignant hymn of hope. It is thought to be a psalm from the period of the Babylonian captivity. The first two verses are a solo part for the psalmist. Eyes are lifted to God in a familiar gesture of humility and expectation. In the vision of the psalmist Israel looks to God just as *slaves* (NIV) or *servants* (NRSV) *and maids* look to *masters* and *mistresses*. The similes are probably appropriate inasmuch as the petition is for mercy (verse 2c).

In verses 3-4 the congregation repeats the plea for mercy, adding its thorough dislike for the contempt the Persian captors are showing. The psalm closes with lines further deploring contempt. Being held in contempt irritated Israel's national sense of self-worth more than almost any other tribulation they were forced to suffer.

God Is on Our Side (Psalm 124)

A victory over persecution is the reason for a joyous tribute to God. The psalmist sings the tribute and bids the congregation repeat it. The tribute is picturesquely embellished in the verses that follow. By the use of some very colorful imagery (verses 3-5), the psalmist paints a gruesome picture of what would have happened without the Lord's having been *on our side.*

The prayer of thanks is a graphic description of the cruel tortures from which God has saved them (verses 6-7). Monsters of the deep with sharp *teeth* would have devoured them and the nets used by bird hunters would have held them captive. Verse 8 is a commonly spoken statement of faith in the liberating presence *(name)* of God.

Zion Abides Forever (Psalm 125)

In the lines of this beautiful little poem are at least three crucial features of Israel's beliefs about what the presence of the Lord means. The first of these (verse 1) is that people who trust God are like the eternally immovable Mount Zion. Their faith is inviolably secure. In verse 2 a second sacred belief is that God's presence means tender care and protection from peril. The beautiful simile of mountains *surround Jerusalem* derives from its picturesque geographic setting. A third essential belief (verse 3) is that no evil will befall their homeland if they, the righteous, are not engaged in wrongdoing.

The recital of these important beliefs is followed by a timely petition to God for gifts to the righteous (verse 4). Verse 5 is an oracle about the fate of the wicked.

God Will Be Faithful (Psalm 126)

The *dream* was that Israel would be restored and *Zion* rebuilt as God's earthly home. In anticipation, the people laughed and sang. Their praise to God was sounded everywhere, even *among the nations* (verse 2). By God's faithfulness, great things have been accomplished.

Now another great thing is needed. Just as the dry *streams* (NIV) or *watercourses* (NRSV) *in the Negeb* are refilled with water annually, so Israel's *fortunes* must be restored (verse 4). Israel's people are sorrowful because of some misfortune, perhaps a drought as implied in the agricultural figures of speech in verses 5-6. Their hope glows in the optimism about a rich harvest (verse 6*b*).

Without God All Is in Vain (Psalm 127)

With this psalm a teacher is illustrating practical wisdom. The importance of God's benevolent presence is beautifully spoken in these popular metaphors of builders and watchmen (verse 1). The lessons continue in verse 2 with the practical advice that working from early morning to late evening will be futile unless God is involved in the effort. The idea that God nurtures our spirits during sleep is also set forth in verse 2.

More proverb-like wisdom is found in verses 4-5. Happy are those who have children. They will continue the family's lineage and provide for the parents in their old age.

Living in Fear of God (Psalm 128)

This is another psalm written by a teacher. Living in fear of the Lord means scrupulous observance of the moral law (precepts, statutes, and ordinances) in every aspect of life. The rewards for faith in these matters are rich indeed. A beatitude for the righteous opens the psalm (verse 1). Verses 2-3 describe the home life of a God-fearing family. Eating the *fruit* of one's *labor* means that those who fear God will not be deprived of what they produce, either by natural disasters or by other actions such as robbery and excessive taxation (verse 2).

More wisdom regarding the family appears in verse 3. The wife will bear many children, like the green olive tree. Numerous sprouts grow from its base. So will such a man be blessed (verse 4).

Verses 5-6 are a priestly blessing. In offering it for the

family which fears God, the priest intentionally includes all of Jerusalem. No family can live in isolation from others and be fully faithful to the name of God. The hope that one may see grandchildren is a splendid metaphor for living a full measure of years. The final word is a benediction seeking *peace* for *Israel*.

A Curse on the Wicked (Psalm 129)

This psalm differs from others in this group in that curses rather than blessings predominate. The reason for the turnabout is found in the first two verses. The psalmist's first words are a vehement denunciation of Israel's persecutors. Despite the persistence of their attacks over the long, sometimes bitter years, they have not been able to demolish the nation (verse 2).

The enemies have caused great suffering. The metaphor of *furrows* suggests the personal punishment of flogging (verse 3). But the *cords* which held Israel in servitude and slavery were *cut* (verse 4). That imagery recalls the release from bondage in Egypt or Babylon.

In the light of this history of persecution, the psalmist prays that Israel's persecutors, those *who hate Zion,* will be destroyed. The simile of grasses compares the evil ones to rooftop weed grasses which struggle for life (verse 6). They differ sharply from the righteous who are likened to good grasses which yield abundant grain (verse 7). Israel believed that the worst thing that can happen to a person is to be denied the blessings of God. Such a curse is wished upon the persecutors.

A Cry from the Depths (Psalm 130)

Interpreters of this psalm are not in agreement about whom the psalmist is representing. Some have suggested it to be Israel. Others think it is an individual in deep distress. Its use in Christian liturgy as a psalm of penitence makes the latter interpretation more appropriate to this commentary. The opening cry (verse

1) comes from the *depths,* a metaphor relating terrible distress to being in the watery deeps. From such a void, the psalmist implores God to listen (verse 2). The cry comes from an admitted sinner; yet if God kept a record (marked *sins* [NIV] *iniquities* [NRSV] no one would be found faultless. For such a one as this sinner, hope lies in God's willingness to forgive (verse 4). So the psalmist *waits* (verse 5) and the waiting is done even more diligently than that of the night watchman who awaits the morning (verse 6).

The climax of this petition for mercy is the expression of confidence and hope. Even though it may have been stimulated by emotional fervor, the petition speaks eloquently to circumstances in Israel's history.

§ § § § § § §

The Message of Psalms 123–130

These psalms deal with concerns of the nation and God's role in mediating the disturbances. In faithfulness to the covenant, God responds and gives Israel hope. The episodes in these psalms generally provide some rationale for Israel's maintenance of a climate of expectancy.

§ There is a limit to Israel's tolerance of its enemies.

§ Israel expects victory because God is with the people.

§ The presence of God liberates the people from persecution and frees them from fear.

§ God will restore Israel again and again.

§ God-fearing people will live successfully.

§ Unless God is present nothing of value can be accomplished.

§ God does punish the wicked.

§ Peace for Israel is not beyond hope.

§ § § § § § §

Psalms 131–140

Introduction to These Psalms

In this part of the Psalms God's attribute of grace tends
to predominate. Although evidence of this gift has not
been lacking in many of the psalms already discussed, we
shall attempt to highlight it here. We do this because of
its special importance to individual persons harboring
anxieties and depression.

A Calm and Quiet Soul (Psalm 131)

This psalm could well have been written by David in
one of his more introspective moods. He becomes
thoroughly attuned to God's moral precepts by avoiding
the sins of pride, arrogance, and conceit (verse 1).
Moreover, he has little interest in trying to impress
people by pretending to be what he is not (verse 1).

In verse 2 David makes it clear that he has come to
terms with life. The lovely simile of mother and child is
David's way of saying that by means of God's grace he
has achieved the ultimate in composure. Verse 3 is an
invitation to the people to share in the great satisfaction
of being in the presence of the God of Israel.

Keep the Covenant (Psalm 132)

The kings of Israel are the principals in this psalm. It
reflects the promises of God to David and his successors.
The psalm is in two parts, both of which have their
historical background in 2 Samuel 7.

The psalmist opens part one (verses 1-10) by recalling

a vow of David to build a *dwelling place* for God. The monologue in verses 1-5 does not have scriptural authority. There is no record in any of the histories that David ever made such a vow. Evidently the story does have some relationship with the capture of the ark by the Philistines (1 Samuel 4:11). The episode described in verses 6-7 deals with the rediscovery of the ark. While the searchers were in Ephrathah (Bethlehem) they received word that the ark was in the fields of Jaar, a village in the hills a few miles west of Jerusalem. They went there and worshiped at the site of the ark, God's *footstool* (verse 7).

In the next stanza (verses 8-10) the ark is returned to the Temple, the appropriate rites are observed, and a successor in David's lineage is anointed king.

The second part of the psalm begins with the psalmist's recollection of God's promise to David that one of his sons would occupy the throne (2 Samuel 7:12-17). The final stanza describes the choice of Zion as God's earthly dwelling. God's presence in Zion will prove to be of great benefit to Israel. The horn to sprout (verse 17) which God will make is the perpetuation of David's lineage as the king of Israel. The *lamp* is that which burns eternally in the Temple as the symbol of an illuminated life. David's *crown* is to bring glory to Israel.

Dwelling in Unity (Psalm 133)

The phrase *when brothers* (NIV) or *kindred* (NRSV) *live together in unity* symbolizes the unity of Israel under the sovereignty of God. It is also a wonderfully *pleasant* experience in the light of Israel's tragic history of brothers in conflict (Cain and Abel, Jacob and Esau, and Absalom and David's other sons). The simile of *oil* on the *beard* (verse 2) has been variously interpreted. It may be only the pleasant aroma of an aromatic oil, or it may refer to the anointing oil of kings administered by a high priest of the order of Aaron. In either case it embellishes the description of happiness.

The simile of the *dew of Hermon* (verse 3) doubtless likens the pleasing unity of brothers to the abundant rainfall associated with Mount Hermon in northern Israel. *There* probably means Zion from which God pronounces life-giving blessings.

Lift Up Your Hands (Psalm 134)

Worshipers are invited to *bless* (NRSV) or *praise* (NIV) the LORD. These people are gathered for evening worship, apparently a regular occurrence. They are then advised to *lift* their *hands,* a gesture of respect to God who resides in the *holy place* (NRSV) or *sanctuary* (NIV). The *holy place* is in the inner court of the Temple. When the act of praise is complete, a priest offers the benediction (verse 3).

God's Mighty Deeds (Psalm 135)

The psalm opens with a familiar call to *praise.* It is addressed to the congregation which has gathered in the courts of the Temple. Two reasons are given for the praise: God is *good* (NIV) *gracious* (NRSV), and God has *chosen* Israel (verses 3-4).

In stanza two, the psalmist sings about mighty acts in the natural world. These acts are the will of God who is above all gods.

The third stanza is a digest of significant episodes in Israel's history from bondage in Egypt to the conquest of Canaan. An account of the *signs and wonders . . . against Pharaoh* is found in Exodus 7-12. God's slaying of *mighty kings, Og* and *Sihon,* is told in Numbers 21:21-35. Their lands subsequently became part of the united Israel.

The psalmist then offers a salutation to the Lord's *name* (verses 13-14). The qualities of divine reliability and *compassion* are singled out for praise. Verses 15-18 describe the inferior quality of other gods made by human hands. The verses are identical to Psalm 115:4-8.

The final stanza is an invitation to *praise*. It is addressed to all of Israel and to the priestly orders of *Aaron* and *Levi*. The two orders served different functions in the rites of temple worship. Those of the order of Aaron dealt primarily with the laity. The order of Levi ministered to and supervised the temple servants and others who were not part of Israel's community of faith. This hymn of praise to the Lord is directed specifically to the intimate presence of God in the geographic, physical center of Israel's religious experience.

God's Great Wonders (Psalm 136)

This is the *Great Hallel* psalm, distinct from the *Little Hallel*, Psalms 113-118. It was written for use during Israel's festivals, particularly Passover, in praise of God's goodness and steadfast love. The content of the psalm is similar to that of Psalm 135, but the literary structure marks it as a choral anthem designed to be sung antiphonally. Congregational participation was doubtless expected because of the refrains being repeated in all twenty-six verses.

The psalm opens with three verses of thanksgiving addressed to God by two different titles. Following this, the psalm repeats the order of Psalm 135, with some variation, in treating important events in Israel's history: the acts of Creation (verses 4-9), bondage in Egypt and the Exodus (verses 10-16), and vanquishing of the Canaanites (verses 17-22).

Verses 23-25 are words of appreciation for God's constant care of Israel during periods of famine, poverty, and assault by vicious enemies. The final verse is a stirring doxology.

The Waters of Babylon (Psalm 137)

The psalm is a reminder that Israel must never forget the tragedy and humiliation of the Exile in Babylon. Those grim days followed the sack of Jerusalem in 587 B.C. (2 Kings 25:1-11).

The *waters of Babylon* are canals along which the captives sat to rest and to remember. The canals were built to divert the flow of the Euphrates River to practical uses in the city. Hanging their *harps* on the *willows* (NRSV) or *poplars* (NIV) that lined the canals was a gesture of defiance. Their captors were ridiculing their beloved sacred songs. It was Babylon's way of taunting them because their God had obviously forgotten all about them (verses 1-3).

The poignancy of their grievous condition is summarized in one plaintive sentence (verse 4) as Israel wonders aloud how it is possible to have sinned so badly that God chose to exile them. It seemed especially unfair because they who survived the trek to Babylon have not forgotten Jerusalem (verse 5).

The final stanza is both a call to remembrance and a curse. In verse 7 God is reminded that the Edomites, descendants of Esau, had abetted Nebuchadnezzar in the destruction of the Temple (Obadiah 10-11). A curse is extended to Babylon which is to suffer some similar indignities (verse 8). The vindictiveness of verse 9 must be understood against the backdrop of centuries of atrocities committed against Israel's people. Captivity and exile were of ancient age. The holocaust was perpetrated in our time.

A Strengthened Soul (Psalm 138)

This is the song of a pious member of the Israelite community of faith. It relates several evidences of God's gift of grace, and verses 1-3 are a personal declaration of thanksgiving. The importance of the occasion to this private person is evident by the emotional fervor of these lines. The inclusion of *gods* (verse 1) is a holdover from Israel's very early experiences before coming to a full understanding of the one God of their monotheistic faith. Thanks are due also because God has graciously given assistance in a time of need (verse 3).

Verses 4-6 demonstrate the psalmist's unusual insight into the special nature of God's grace. Kings praise the greatness and glory of God. Yet God holds the haughty and the proud among them at a distance while embracing those of lesser estate in a radiant presence. The psalmist has learned what God's presence means to the private person. When in the midst of trouble such a person will have as much support from God as kings (verse 7). From the depths of faith the assurance is felt that God's purpose for the psalmist's life will be fulfilled. The petition in verse 8c seeks God's continuous care.

Whither Shall I Go? (Psalm 139)

This is one of the great devotional psalms as well as a priceless literary gem circulated well beyond the Psalter. This psalm can best be understood as a very private prayer in which God and the reader are very much alone. The content differs sharply from the other psalms in this group. It does not deal with history or God's actions in Israel's behalf. On the contrary, this psalm is fully contemporary for any era and the text is largely self-explanatory.

The first stanza (verses 1-6) is an acknowledgment of God's immediate awareness of the psalmist's thoughts. Human comprehension of powers of this kind is impossible. Divine foreknowledge of every thought makes it impossible to hide from God's presence (verses 7-12). The idea that God can go to Sheol contradicts the general belief that *Sheol* (NRSV; NIV= *depths*) is a place God does not visit. The *wings of the morning* (NRSV) or *dawn* (NIV) is a metaphor of the Canaanite mythological winged goddess of dawn.

In verses 13-18 the psalmist muses on the wonders of God's creation of the human form. The language is not only beautiful but surprisingly accurate. Verses 15-16 are uncommonly perceptive in their treatment of God's creative processes through millennia of biological development. Verses 19-22 are the psalmist's vigorous reaction to enemies who are known to be God's enemies as well. This lovely psalm closes with a prayer for guidance.

Deliver Us from Evil (Psalm 140)

This psalm is one of very few in the Psalter which are not redemptive in some way. It is a petition for retribution, somewhat vengeful and violent. The psalm begins with a typical cry for help. It is followed by a description of the enemies' actions (verses 2-3). Another plea is sounded (verse 4) at which point the psalmist praises God for assistance (verses 6-7) and asks that the enemies be restrained (verse 8).

Rather hideous retribution is sought for the enemies (verses 9-11). In the final verses (12-13) the psalmist affirms God's concern for the needy. The tone of these verses suggests that the psalmist may be seeking self-reassurance.

§ § § § § § §

The Message of Psalms 131–140

The repetitive use of *Bless the* LORD in this group of psalms is to emphasize Israel's faithfulness. The blessing is also spoken with some expectation that God's grace will be manifested in all that transpires.

§ God's grace enables one to accept life as it unfolds.

§ God's grace informs the actions of kings.

§ God's grace is manifested by the divine presence in Jerusalem on Mount Zion.

§ God's grace is manifested to Israel by the saving acts in the nation's history.

§ God's grace provides steadfast love for Israel.

§ God's grace has enabled Israel to bear its burdens, even the most calamitous.

§ God's grace sustains the lowly as well as kings.

§ Grace allows for private time to commune with God.

§ § § § § § §

Psalms 141–150

Introduction to These Psalms

The psalms in this final part are chiefly songs of loving adoration, praise, and thanksgiving. They are addressed to God who gave diligent oversight to the preservation of Israel as a nation. This oversight continues in our time despite gaps of hundreds of years. These psalms are not formal Hallel songs of praise (see Psalms 113–118; 136), but they acknowledge God as the exhilarating core around which all of Israel's life swirls. The last five psalms (146–150) are identified as the *hallelujah psalms* because of the frequency of the words *Praise the* LORD.

Guide Me Aright (Psalm 141)

The typical cry for help opens this psalm, but after verse 1 it departs from the lament. In verse 2 the psalmist offers a winsome prayer with the traditional Temple rites in mind. An effective metaphor of a *guard* on the *lips* petitions God to limit the psalmist's speech to righteous things (verse 3). God is also asked to be the guardian of the psalmist's thoughts, lest they drift toward evil persons and the temptations they would offer (verse 4).

The psalmist is not unwilling to be criticized by righteous people but wants nothing to do with the wicked who, in due time, will learn that what God says is true (verses 5-6). Then, in a sudden change of mood, the psalmist hurls a death wish at the wicked (verse 7).

With another abrupt change in tone the psalmist turns to God, seeking refuge and protection from *snares* (NIV) or *trap* (NRSV) (verse 9). But, in the final verse, vindictiveness creeps in and the psalmist is unable to resist pronouncing a curse.

A Voice from Prison (Psalm 142)

An all-knowing God is already aware of this poor prisoner who has uttered a piteous cry for help (verses 1-3a). The distress is caused by persecutors who are tormenting the prisoner unmercifully. Unfortunately, there is no one around who will restrain them (verses 3b-4).

The cry for help is repeated with some acknowledgment that God is a helper. The plea is based on the knowledge that without help this prisoner will be overwhelmed by these insufferable people (verses 5-6).

In verse 7 God is requested simply to remove the prisoner from bondage so that praise may be offered. Implicit faith suggests that the prisoner will then be able to live among the righteous. Praise the Lord!

A Soul Thirsts for God (Psalm 143)

This psalm is the penitent prayer of a sinner. The appeal is for mercy. Although the psalmist has been hounded by an enemy and pressured almost to the point of death (verse 3), the problem is personal sinfulness. Evidence of the latter is the request to God to make no *judgment* (verse 2). If this poor psalmist were to be tried in the heavenly court, nothing but a guilty verdict could be rendered. The psalmist's reasoning is that no person could ever be proved fully righteous before God.

Recalling Israel's history and God's saving grace, the psalmist appeals to God for mercy (verses 5-6). The petition continues, pleading for haste lest the next stop be the *Pit* (verse 7). Prayers such as these were frequently offered in the evening with the expectation that God would provide a response by the following morning (verse 8a). Verse 8b suggests a serious commitment to a life of righteousness. Having made the commitment, the psalmist seeks deliverance, wisdom (God's *will*), and guidance along a *level path* (NRSV) or *ground* (NIV) (verses 9-10). The psalm closes with a plea for mercy and a curse on the *adversaries* (NRSV) or *foes* (NIV).

Two Poems (Psalm 144)

This psalm has two sections, the first being the rambling discourse of a warrior king. Section two is a prayer of thanksgiving for economic prosperity. The psalm opens with a blessing on God who teaches the arts of war and who is the king's *refuge* and *shield* (verses 1-2). Musing on the nature of humans (see Psalm 8:4), the king concludes that humanity is transitory.

The next stanza is the king's appeal to God to reveal divine authority by mighty deeds in the world (verses 5-6). The king also seeks relief from the flood of *many waters* (enemies) and *lies* from the lips of *aliens* (verses 7-11).

In this second section, the psalmist portrays a well-ordered, prosperous, and healthy household. It may be symbolic of hope for Israel's future. The similes for *sons* and *daughters* (verse 12) also suggest hope for a rich future. The barns are full after the harvest is over (verse 13). There will be no breaching in the walls means no miscarriage or spontaneous abortion (verse 14). The psalm closes with beatitudes of praise to God.

The Lord Is Near (Psalm 145)

This psalm is one of the Psalter's great masterpieces, not especially for literary merit but moreso for the scope of its content. It is a remarkably comprehensive summary of Israel's understanding of what God's universal sovereignty means. Through the psalm, numerous divine characteristics are identified. The psalmist begins by offering both blessing and *praise* to God's *name* (verses 1-2).

By acknowledging that God's *greatness is unsearchable* (NRSV) or *no one can fathom* (NRSV) (verse 3), the psalmist is suggesting that, despite the wonders of what is to follow, there is no way that the depths of God's love and generosity can ever be told.

A sentence of hope follows to the effect that future generations will praise God endlessly for *mighty acts.* These are the major episodes that have been Israel's salvation. The psalmist then mentions God's *majesty* and also wondrous works, an all-encompassing subject suitable for meditation (verses 4-5). *Awesome deeds* of verse 6 are those causing terror in the hearts of enemies of the people as well as the wicked. *Goodness and righteousness* are equally deserving of praise (verse 7).

In stanza three the psalmist says God is *gracious, merciful* (NRSV), and *compassionate* (NIV). Also admitted to the list of God's attributes are forbearance *(slow to anger)* and *rich in love* (NIV) *steadfast love* (NRSV), In the stanza following, the psalmist observes that saints or the faithful shall bless God for glory of God's kingdom, power, and mighty deeds. Moreover the kingdom endures.

Stanza four (verses 13c-20) records additional characteristics which are, apart from being *faithful* (verse 13c), God's ministry to the material needs of the people. Included are the support of the oppressed (verse 14), an adequate *food* supply (verse 15), and the satisfaction of the *desire* of all God's creatures (verse 16).

The psalmist continues this splendid register by adding justice and kindness (verse 17), responsiveness to any cry for help, and especially being *near* (verse 17-19). The last of the attributes to be described is God's promise of salvation (verse 20). God's willingness to destroy the wicked is also included. The psalm ends with a call to praise of God's *holy name.*

Trust Not in Princes (Psalm 146)

This psalm is the first of the five great *Hallelujah* poems which bring the Psalter to a close. *Hallelujah* means *praise ye the LORD.* It is derived from the Hebrew *hallel* (praise) and *Yah,* the first syllable of the Hebrew word for God, Yahweh. The opening verses are the psalmist's own words of glorious praise, full of the consuming love of God.

The theme of the psalm is set forth in verses 3-4.

Princes of the world can never provide what God can in order to help Israel achieve its destiny. True happiness is achieved only when trust and hope are centered in God. The Creator's characteristics of faithfulness, justice, and sustenance for the poor and the hungry are stressed (verses 6-7). Among the most beautiful sentiments in all of the Scripture are those in verses 7c-9b. No commentary could ever improve nor could interpretation add to them. What better reason to praise the Lord?

Verse 9c, like Psalm 145:20b, represents a problem for some students of the Psalter. However, these expressions of vindictiveness are understandable in view of the atrocities committed against Israel throughout her history.

Verse 10 is the praise of a psalmist whose life is victorious in the ways of the Lord.

Praise God, O Zion (Psalm 147)

The second of the hallelujah psalms is a three-stanza treatment of the praise theme using familiar aspects of God's special relationship with Israel. In stanza one, following the customary words of *praise* (verse 1), the psalmist compares distinctively different examples of God's wondrous works. That God who made the stars (verse 4), would care for the *outcasts* (NRSV) or *exiles* (NIV) *of Israel* and the heartbroken (verses 2-3), and lift the oppressed (verse 6) is ample cause for praise.

Stanza two has a similar motif. The God who is in control of all nature (verse 8) and who cares for the livelihood of animals without requiring special praise (verses 9-10) is also the God who takes pleasure in knowing that Israel respects and reveres her God.

The third stanza opens with praise to God for attending to the security of Zion and the protection of the citizens of Jerusalem (verses 12-13). God is also praised as the architect of *peace* for Israel and for benevolent oversight of its agriculture (verse 15).

The psalmist's descriptions of weather (verses 15-18) illustrate God's ultimate control of nature. It is perceived by Israel as evidence of a divine will (verses 15-18). Verse 19 takes account of God's selection of Israel *(Jacob)* as the chosen people. *Praise the LORD!*

God's Name Is Exalted (Psalm 148)

This lyrical psalm of praise consists of two parts. In part one (verses 1-7) the call to praise is addressed to the fixtures of heaven and the heavenly host. The call in part two (verses 8-14) is addressed to earth.

Praise from heaven is to recognize God's creation and regulation of the celestial universe and the company of angels. Praise from earth is to acknowledge God's creation and command of the earth's geography and all living creatures (verses 9-10). God's special creation, humanity, is also called to praise irrespective of station in life, whether kings or children (verses 11-12).

All are summoned, but the special relationship between God and Israel is noted in verse 14. *Horn* is symbolic of Israel's dignified role in God's plan.

Let Israel Be Glad (Psalm 149)

The psalm is a hallelujah poem sung in praise of God. The occasion for its composition was the celebration of a victory over distress of considerable importance. All Israel is invited to praise the *King*. In this instance it is God who is the victorious warrior king (verses 2, 4). The people are invited to continue their praise during their hours of repose and perhaps refreshment (verse 5).

Within verse 6 the psalm becomes one of vengeance. The *double-edged* (NIV) or *two-edged sword* (NRSV; verse 6b) is not the common figure of speech here. It is the weapon to be used on the enemy nations as Israel executes the *sentence* (NIV) decreed in God's *judgment* (NRSV) (verse 9). The vengeance here differs from the vindictiveness of Psalms 137 and 147. What is at issue is not the matter of atrocities but Israel's belief that she is commissioned by God to fight holy wars against oppressor nations which do not revere Israel's living God.

Praise the Lord (Psalm 150)

This lovely poem which closes the book of Psalms hardly requires commentary. It is the inspirational psalm of psalms for a worshiping congregation. The *sanctuary* of verse 1 is the house of God anywhere God's people gather, anywhere under the spacious *firmament* (NRSV) or *heavens* (NIV). *Mighty deeds* (NRSV) or *acts of power* (NIV) have been eloquently portrayed throughout the Psalter. Creations of the universe and the moral law come to mind as do the saving acts of redemption of God's people everywhere. Praise by everything that breathes is praise incomparable. Accolades to God's glorious universe could not be better spoken. *Praise the* LORD!

§ § § § § § §

The Message of Psalms 141–150

The invitation to praise the Lord appears throughout the Psalms a hundred times or more. Praise is the predominant way Israel expressed its faithfulness to God. It seems appropriate that the last chapters of the Psalter are given over to extensive praise *(Hallelujah)*.

§ Praise God for moral guidance.
§ Praise God for mercy and for salvation.
§ Praise God for always being near in times of need.
§ Praise God for grace and compassion.
§ Praise God for freeing prisoners, healing the sick, and lifting the oppressed.
§ Praise God for the care of widows and orphans.
§ Praise God for bounteous harvests.
§ Praise God for the special care of Israel.

§ § § § § § §

Glossary of Terms

Aaron: A priest of Israel; brother of Miriam and Moses.
Abaddon: Literally, *destruction;* the depths of Sheol.
Abarim: A hilly area in Moab east of the Dead Sea.
Abimelech: A Canaanite king; a contemporary of Abraham.
Abraham: The first patriarch of Israel, whose name was changed from Abram.
Absalom: A son of David who conspired to overthrow his father, the king; Absalom was slain in the conflict.
Ahimelech: A priest of Israel; a contemporary of David.
Alamoth: Literally, young women. In the psalm title, it may indicate a song for women's voices.
Ammon: A land east of Palestine over the Jordan River.
Amorites: A people of early Canaanite origin.
Asaph: A chief musician of David's court. The *sons of Asaph* may be members of a guild of singers dating from the period of the monarchy.
Ascents: A *Song of Ascent;* a psalm which was sung by pilgrims ascending the slopes of the hill of Zion.
Assyria: The dominant civilization of Mesopotamia prior to 612 B.C. when it was destroyed by Babylon.
Baal: A Canaanite fertility god.
Babylon: The successor civilization to Assyria in Mesopotamia; absorbed by Persia in 539 B.C.
Baca: An imaginary valley of sorrows.
Bashan: An area northeast of the Sea of Galilee.
Benjaminite: A member of the tribe of Benjamin, the younger son of Jacob and Rachel; brother of Joseph.

Canaan: The ancient land of central Palestine which was chosen by God for Israel.

Cush: A land south of Egypt also known as Ethiopia.

Edom: A region south of Palestine ranging from the Dead Sea to Sinai and the Red Sea.

Edomites: The people of Edom; descended from Esau.

Endor: A village of Palestine south of Mount Tabor.

Ephraim: A son of Joseph; leader of a tribe bearing his name.

Ethan: Probably a singer in the tradition of Levi.

Ethiopia: A land south of Egypt known also as Cush.

Gilead: A tribe of Israel situated east of the Jordan River and south of the Sea of Galilee.

Gittith: A word having to do with instrumental music.

Ham: The second son of Noah and the ancestor of the peoples of northeast Africa.

Hermon: A mountain in Syria; also known as Sirion.

Higgaion: Literally, a solemn musical sound.

Horeb: A mountain in the Sinai peninsula; also known as Mount Sinai.

Isaac: Son of Abraham and Sarah; patriarch of Israel.

Ishmaelites: The descendants of Ishmael, son of Abraham and Hagar.

Israel: The people of the Psalms originating with Jacob and the twelve tribes.

Jaar: A village several miles west of Jerusalem.

Jacob: Son of Isaac; father of sons who became the leaders of the twelve tribes; Jacob is also used as a synonym for Israel.

Jeduthun: A singer in the tradition of Levi.

Jehoiachin: King of Israel at the time of the Babylonian invasion and sack of Jerusalem.

Jerusalem: Capital city of Israel; God's home in Zion.

Jesse: Son of Obed; father of David; member of the tribe of Judah.

Joab: A nephew of David; a brilliant miltary strategist.

Jordan River: The major river of Palestine flowing from Lebanon in the far north to the Dead Sea.

Joseph: The son of Jacob and Rachel; older brother of Benjamin.

Judah: Fourth son of Jacob; one of the twelve tribes of Israel.

Kadesh: An oasis in the desert of the Sinai peninsula.

Kedar: A place in the desert land east of Palestine; a wandering people, probably Ishmaelites.

Korah: Great-grandson of Levi; the word may also be the name of a guild of Temple singers dating back to Levi and the priestly, musical traditions.

Leannoth: An antiphonal performance by two choral groups.

Lebanon: The region north of Palestine between Syria and the Mediterranean coast.

Levi: The third son of Jacob; associated with the origin of the Levitical priesthood and Temple music.

Leviathan: A mythological dragon subdued by God at Creation.

Lilies: Probably the name of a tune.

Mahalath: Probably the name of a tune.

Manasseh: The first son of Joseph; a tribe of Israel.

Maskil: The meaning is uncertain; it may be a meditation.

Massah and Meribah: A place on Mount Horeb where water was brought forth from a rock. (Psalm 81)

Melchizedek: A priest-king in Salem (Jerusalem); a contemporary of Abraham.

Meshech: A people and a place in Asia Minor between the Black and the Caspian Seas.

Miktam: The meaning is uncertain; it may indicate an atonement psalm.

Moab: A land immediately east of the Dead Sea and south of the River Arnon.

Muth-labben: Probably the name of a tune or a musical instruction.

Naphtali: The sixth son of Jacob; one of the twelve tribes.

Nathan: A prophet in the court of David; perhaps a chronicler of the Davidic events.

Og: The king of Bashan.

Ophir: An area of the Arabian coast of the Red Sea.

Peor: A mountain in Moab; in biblical literature, an early Canaanite god, Baal-peor.

Philistia: A land in western Israel on the coast of the Mediterranean Sea.

Philistines: The people of Philistia; they originated somewhere in Greece.

Phinehas: A grandson of Aaron; chief priest of Israel and a contemporary of Joshua.

Pit: A synonym of Sheol.

Rahab: A mytholgogical dragon slain by God at Creation; also a literary synonym for Egypt.

Saul: The first king of the united Israel.

Seba: A kingdom somewhere in Cush (Ethiopia).

Selah: See the Introduction to the Psalms, page 12.

Sheba: A kingdom of northwest Arabia.

Shechem: A city of Manasseh north of Jerusalem.

Sheminith: Probably a musical instruction.

Sheol: The third and lowest tier of the universe made up of heaven, earth and Sheol.

Shiggaion: An emotional, passionate song.

Shushan Eduth: Probably the name of a psalm.

Sihon: An Amorite king living in Hesbon east of the Jordan River.

Sinai: A mountain; also a peninsula of land between Palestine and Egypt.

Sisera: A Canaanite king who was slain during Israel's conquest of the promised land.

Solomon: The son of David and Bathsheba; the builder of the first great Temple in Jerusalem.

Tabor: Mountain in Palestine southwest of the Sea of Galilee.

Tarshish: A city probably situated on the southeast coast of what is modern-day Spain.

Terebinths: A species of gum trees; the turpentine tree of the middle east.

Tyre: A city of Lebanon on the Mediterranean coast.

Zalmunna and Zebah: Midianite kings slain by Gideon who was avenging the murder of his brothers.

Zebulun: The tenth son of Jacob; one of the twelve tribes.

Zion: A hill in Jerusalem; the earthly home of God; also used as a synonym of Jerusalem.

Ziphites: A clan of the tribe of Judah.

Guide to Pronunciation

Abaddon: Ah-BAD-dun
Abarim: Ah-bah-REEM
Abimelech: Ah-BIM-uh-leck
Ahimelech: Ah-HIM-uh-leck
Alamoth: AL-uh-moth
Amalek: AM-uh-leck
Aram-nahaaraim: AIR-am-Nah-har-uh-EEM
Aram-zobah: AIR-um-ZOH-bah
Asaph: AY-saff
Assyria: Ah-SEER-ee-ah
Baal: Bah-ALL
Baca: Bah-KAH
Bashan: Bah-SHAHN
Dathan: Dah-THAHN
Doeg: DOH-egg
Endor: EN-door
Ephraim: Ee-frah-EEM
Ephraimites: EE-frah-eem-ites
Ephrathah: EFF-ra-thah
Ethiopia: Ee-thee-OPE-ee-ah
Ezrahite: EZ-rah-hite
Gebal: GAY-ball
Gittith: GIT-tith
Hagarites: HAY-guh-rites
Higgaion: HIG-eye-on
Horeb: HOR-ebb
Ishmaelites: ISH-may-eh-lites

Jaar: Jah-ARE
Jabin: JAY-bin
Jeduthun: JED-uh-thun
Jehoiachin: Jeh-HOY-ah-kin
Kadesh: KAY-desh
Kedar: KEY-dar
Kishion: KISH-ee-un
Leannoth: LEE-un-noth
Leviathan: Luh-VIE-uh-thun
Mahalath: Mah-hah-LAHTH
Manasseh: Muh-NASS-uh
Maskil: MAHS-kil
Massah: MAH-suh
Melchizedek: Mel-KIH-zuh-dek
Meribah: MARE-uh-bah
Meshech: MEE-shek
Miktam: MICK-tam
Muth-labben: MUTH-lab-un
Naphtali: Naff-TAH-lee
Ophir: OH-fear
Oreb: OR-ebb
Peor: Pea-ORE
Philistia: Fill-ISS-tee-ah
Phinehas: Fih-NAY-has
Selah: Seh-LAH
Shechem: SHECK-um
Sheminith: SHEM-uh-nith
Shiggaion: SHIG-eye-on
Shushan Eduth: SHOE-shan-EE-doth
Sihon: SEE-hun
Sinai: SIGH-nye
Sirion: SEER-ee-un
Sisera: SIS-eh-rah
Succoth: SUK-uth
Tarshish: TAR-shish
Terebinths: TEAR-uh-binths
Ziphites: ZIF-ites

Concordance of Familiar Phrases

Keep me as the apple of your eye. (17:8*a* NIV)
Guard me as the apple of the eye. (17:8*a* NRSV)
Praise the LORD, O my soul. (103:1 NIV)
Bless the LORD, O my soul. (103:1 NRSV)
How good and pleasant it is/ when brothers live together in unity! (133:1 NIV)
How very good and pleasant it is/ when kindred live together in unity! (133:1 NRSV)
Cast your cares on the LORD. (55:22 NIV)
Cast your burden on the LORD. (55:22 NRSV)
The cattle on a thousand hills. (50:10 NIV and NRSV)
Better is one day in your courts/ than a thousand elsewhere. (84:10 NIV)
For a day in your courts is better/ than a thousand elsewhere. (84:10 NRSV)
Create in me a pure heart, O God. (51:10 NIV)
Create in me a clean heart, O God. (51:10 NRSV)
My cup overflows. (23:5 NIV and NRSV)
Deep calls to deep. (42:7 NIV and NRSV)
Out of the depths I cry to you, O LORD. (130:1 NIV and NRSV)
Out to the sea in ships. (107:23 NIV)
Down to the sea in ships. (107:23 NRSV)
As far as the east is from the west,/ so far has he removed our transgressions from us. (103:12 NIV)
As far as the east is from the west,/ so far he removes our transgressions from us. (103:12 NRSV)
From everlasting to everlasting you are God. (90:2 NIV and NRSV)
The fear of the LORD is the beginning of wisdom. (111:10 NIV and NRSV)
"Flee like a bird to your mountain." (11:1 NIV)
"Flee like a bird to the mountains." (11:1 NRSV)
The fool says in his heart,/ "There is no God." (14:1 NIV)

Fools say in their hearts, "There is no God." (14:1 NRSV)

My God, my God, why have you forsaken me? (22:1 NIV and NRSV)

He alone is my rock and my salvation;/ he is my fortress, I will never be shaken. (62:2 NIV)

He alone is my rock and my salvation,/ my fortress; I shall never be shaken. (62:2 NRSV)

I rejoiced with those who said to me,/ "Let us go to the house of the LORD." (122:1 NIV)

I was glad when they said to me,/ "Let us go to the house of the LORD!" (122:1 NRSV)

It is good to praise the LORD. (92:1 NIV)

It is good to give thanks to the LORD. (92:1 NRSV)

May God be gracious to us and bless us/ and make his face shine upon us. (67:1 NIV)

May God be gracious to us and bless us/ and make his face to shine upon us. (67:1 NRSV)

Great is the LORD and most worthy of praise. (145:3 NIV)

Great is the LORD, and greatly to be praised. (145:3 NRSV)

For as high as the heavens are above the earth,/ so great is his love for those who fear him. (103:11 NIV)

For as the heavens are high above the earth,/ so great is his steadfast love toward those who fear him. (103:11 NRSV)

Our help is in the name of the LORD,/ the Maker of heaven and earth. (124:8 NIV)

Our help is in the name of the LORD,/ who made heaven and earth. (124:8 NRSV)

Your word is a lamp to my feet/ and a light for my path. (119:105 NIV)

Your word is a lamp to my feet/ and a light to my path. (119:105 NRSV)

The law of the LORD is perfect. (19:7 NIV and NRSV)

Lead me in the way everlasting. (139:24 NIV and NRSV)

May the peoples praise you, O God. (67:3 NIV)

Let the peoples praise you, O God. (67:3 NRSV)

May the words of my mouth and the meditation of my heart/ be pleasing in your sight. (19:14 NIV)

Let the words of my mouth and the meditation of my heart/ be acceptable to you. (19:14 NRSV)

I lift up my eyes to the hills. (121:1 NIV and NRSV)

Send forth your light and your truth. (43:3 NIV)

O send out your light and your truth. (43:3 NRSV)

The LORD is compassionate and gracious,/ slow to anger, abounding in love. (103:8 NIV)

The LORD is merciful and gracious,/ slow to anger and abounding in steadfast love. (103:8 NRSV)

The LORD is in his holy temple. (11:4a NIV and NRSV)

The LORD reigns, let the earth be glad. (97:1 NIV)

The LORD is king! Let the earth rejoice. (97:1 NRSV)

The LORD will keep you from all harm. (121:7 NIV)

The LORD will keep you from all evil. (121:7 NRSV)

From everlasting to everlasting/ the LORD's love is with those who fear him. (103:17 NIV)

The steadfast love of the LORD/ is from everlasting to everlasting/ on those who fear him. (103:17 NRSV)

From the lips of children and infants . . . (8:2 NIV)

Out of the mouths of babes and infants . . . (8:2 NRSV)

Shout with joy to God, all the earth! (66:1 NIV and NRSV)

The God of Jacob is our fortress. (46:7 NIV)

The God of Jacob is our refuge. (46:7 NRSV)

God is our refuge and strength,/ an ever-present help in trouble. (46:1 NIV)

God is our refuge and strength,/ a very present help in trouble. (46:1 NRSV)

Lead me to the rock that is higher than I. (61:2 NIV and NRSV)

Search me, O God, and know my heart. (139:23 NIV and NRSV)

Hide me in the shadow of your wings. (17:8b NIV and NRSV)

If the LORD had not been on our side . . . (124:1 NIV)

If it had not been the LORD who was on our side . . . (124:1 NRSV)

Indeed, he who watches over Israel/ will neither slumber nor sleep. (121:4 NIV)

He who keeps Israel will neither slumber nor sleep. (121:4 NRSV)

Teach us to number our days aright,/ that we may gain a heart of wisdom. (90:12 NIV)

So teach us to count our days/ that we may gain a wise heart. (90:12 NRSV)

My soul waits for the Lord. (130:6 NIV and NRSV)

The stone the builders rejected/ has become the capstone. (118:22 NIV)

The stone that the builders rejected/ has become the chief cornerstone. (118:22 NRSV)

All your words are true;/ all your righteous laws are eternal. (119:160 NIV)

The sum of your word is truth;/ and every one of your righteous ordinances endures forever. (119:160 NRSV)

How sweet are your words to my taste,/ sweeter than honey to my mouth! (119:103 NIV and NRSV)

Teach me your decrees. (119:135 NIV)

Teach me your statutes. (119:135 NRSV)

The heavens declare the glory of God. (19:1 NIV)

The heavens are telling the glory of God. (19:1 NRSV)

My times are in your hands. (31:15 NIV)

My times are in your hand. (31:15 NRSV)

Do not put your trust in princes. (146:3 NIV and NRSV)

Unless the LORD builds the house,/ its builders labor in vain. (127:1 NIV)

Unless the LORD builds the house,/ those who build it labor in vain. (127:1 NRSV)

Wash me, and I will be whiter than snow. (51:7 NIV)

Wash me, and I shall be whiter than snow. (51:7 NRSV)

Where can I go from your Spirit? (139:7 NIV)

Where can I go from your spirit? (139:7 NRSV)

If I rise on the wings of the dawn . . . (139:9 NIV)

If I take the wings of the morning . . . (139:9 NRSV)

"Oh, that I had the wings of a dove!" (55:6 NIV)

"O that I had wings like a dove!" (55:6 NRSV)

They were at their wits' end. (107:27 NIV)

[They] were at their wits' end. (107:27 NRSV)

The length of our days is seventy years. (90:10 NIV)

The days of our life are seventy years. (90:10 NRSV)

For a thousand years in your sight/ are like a day that has just gone by,/ or like a watch in the night. (90:4 NIV)

For a thousand years in your sight/ are like yesterday when it is past,/ or like a watch in the night. (90:4 NRSV)